Project 2025

Meets

Agenda 47

Aligning National Priorities and Policies

Richard B. Romney

Dedication

To my family, whose unwavering support and love have been my greatest inspiration. You have been my guiding light throughout this journey.

Table of Contents

Introduction to Project 2025

Project 2025 is a strategic initiative by the Heritage Foundation, aimed at preparing conservative leaders and policy experts for potential future governance. The project is designed to ensure that conservative principles and policies are effectively implemented in the federal government, with a focus on the year 2025 as a pivotal moment for conservative leadership in America.

Goals and Vision

Project 2025 is built on several key objectives:

1. **Preparing Conservative Leaders**: The initiative seeks to identify, train, and place conservative leaders in key positions within the federal government. This includes preparing individuals who are committed to upholding conservative values and can effectively navigate the complexities of federal bureaucracy.

2. **Policy Development and Implementation**: The project aims to develop comprehensive policy proposals that align with conservative principles. These policies are intended to address critical issues facing the nation, including economic growth, national security, healthcare, education, and more.

3. **Restoring Constitutional Governance**: A core goal of Project 2025 is to restore governance according to the U.S. Constitution. This includes reducing the size and scope of the federal government, promoting states' rights, and ensuring that all government actions are constitutionally sound.

Key Components of Project 2025

Project 2025 comprises several key components, each designed to address different aspects of governance and policy implementation:

1. **The Conservative Governance Task Force**: This task force is responsible for identifying and vetting potential candidates for key positions within the federal government. The goal is to ensure that these individuals are well-prepared to implement conservative policies effectively.

2. **Policy Working Groups**: These groups bring together policy experts from various fields to develop detailed policy proposals. Each working group focuses on a specific area, such as economic policy, national security, healthcare, or education, and works to create actionable plans that can be implemented by a future conservative administration.

3. **Training Programs**: Project 2025 includes extensive training programs for future leaders. These programs cover a wide range of topics, including leadership skills, policy development, and the workings of the federal government. The aim is to equip conservative leaders with the knowledge and skills they need to succeed in government roles.

4. **Research and Analysis**: The Heritage Foundation conducts in-depth research and analysis to support Project 2025. This research covers a broad array of topics and provides the evidence base for the policy proposals developed by the working groups.

Detailed Policy Areas

Project 2025 addresses a wide range of policy areas, each with specific goals and proposed actions:

1. **Economic Policy**

    o **Tax Reform**: Simplifying the tax code, reducing tax rates, and eliminating unnecessary regulations to spur economic growth and increase job creation.

- o **Spending Cuts**: Reducing federal spending by eliminating wasteful programs and implementing fiscal discipline to reduce the national debt.

- o **Deregulation**: Rolling back excessive regulations that hinder business growth and innovation, particularly in key industries such as energy, technology, and finance.

2. **National Security and Defense**

- o **Military Strength**: Enhancing military capabilities through increased funding, modernization of equipment, and strategic realignment of forces.

- o **Cybersecurity**: Strengthening national cybersecurity infrastructure to protect against cyber threats and ensure the security of critical systems.

- o **Border Security**: Implementing robust measures to secure the nation's borders, including increased border patrols, advanced surveillance technology, and comprehensive immigration reform.

3. **Healthcare Reform**

- o **Patient-Centered Care**: Promoting healthcare policies that prioritize patient choice, affordability, and quality of care.

- o **Market-Based Solutions**: Encouraging competition in the healthcare market to drive down costs and improve services.

- o **Medicare and Medicaid Reform**: Reforming these programs to ensure their long-term sustainability and efficiency.

4. **Education and Workforce Development**

- o **School Choice**: Expanding options for parents and students through charter schools, voucher programs, and homeschooling initiatives.

- o **Curriculum Reform**: Promoting a curriculum that emphasizes civic education, STEM subjects, and vocational training.

- o **Workforce Training**: Developing programs that equip workers with the skills needed for the modern economy, particularly in high-demand fields such as technology and manufacturing.

5. **Energy and Environment**

- o **Energy Independence**: Promoting domestic energy production through the development of fossil fuels, nuclear energy, and renewable resources.

- o **Environmental Stewardship**: Implementing policies that balance economic growth with environmental protection, encouraging conservation and sustainable practices.

- o **Regulatory Reform**: Streamlining environmental regulations to reduce the burden on businesses while ensuring protection of natural resources.

6. **Judicial and Legal Reforms**

- o **Judicial Appointments**: Appointing judges who adhere to a strict interpretation of the Constitution and respect the rule of law.

- o **Legal Reforms**: Implementing reforms to reduce frivolous lawsuits, protect property rights, and ensure a fair and efficient legal system.

- o **Criminal Justice**: Enhancing public safety through effective law enforcement, fair sentencing, and rehabilitation programs.

Implementation Strategy

Project 2025 outlines a detailed strategy for implementing these policies, focusing on the following areas:

1. **Federal Appointments**: Identifying and placing qualified individuals in key positions within the federal government to ensure effective policy implementation.

2. **Legislative Agenda**: Working with Congress to pass legislation that supports the goals of Project 2025. This includes building coalitions, lobbying efforts, and public advocacy.

3. **Public Engagement**: Engaging with the American public to build support for conservative policies. This includes grassroots organizing, media campaigns, and community outreach.

4. **Monitoring and Evaluation**: Continuously monitoring the progress of policy implementation and evaluating the impact of these policies. This ensures accountability and allows for adjustments as needed.

Project 2025 represents a comprehensive and ambitious plan by the Heritage Foundation to prepare for and influence future conservative governance in America. By focusing on leadership development, detailed policy proposals, and strategic implementation, the initiative aims to strengthen America's position on the world stage and ensure that conservative principles guide the nation's future direction. The success of Project 2025 depends on the collaborative efforts of policymakers, leaders, and the American public to achieve these transformative goals.

Overview of Agenda 47

Agenda 47 is a comprehensive policy blueprint put forth by Donald Trump, reflecting his vision for America's future. Building on his previous presidency, Agenda 47 outlines a strategic plan aimed at restoring American greatness through bold economic policies, strong national defense, and a commitment to conservative values. This agenda seeks to address the challenges facing the nation while capitalizing on opportunities to ensure long-term prosperity and security for all Americans.

Key Objectives of Agenda 47

1. **Economic Revival**

   o **Tax Reform**: One of the central pillars of Agenda 47 is comprehensive tax reform aimed at stimulating economic growth. This includes reducing individual and corporate tax rates, simplifying the tax code, and eliminating loopholes that favor special interests.

   o **Job Creation**: A major focus is on creating jobs across various sectors, particularly manufacturing, technology, and energy. This involves promoting policies that encourage domestic production and investment.

   o **Deregulation**: Reducing the regulatory burden on businesses is seen as crucial for economic growth. Agenda 47 advocates for rolling back unnecessary regulations that stifle innovation and entrepreneurship.

2. **Strengthening National Security**

   o **Military Modernization**: Ensuring that the U.S. military remains the most powerful in the world is a key priority. This includes increased funding for defense, investment in advanced technology, and modernization of military infrastructure.

   o **Border Security**: Enhancing border security is central to Agenda 47, with a focus on building stronger barriers, increasing the number of border patrol agents, and utilizing advanced surveillance technology.

- o **Counterterrorism**: Strengthening efforts to combat terrorism both domestically and internationally through intelligence sharing, military action, and alliances with global partners.

3. **Healthcare Reform**

   - o **Patient-Centered Care**: Agenda 47 emphasizes reforming the healthcare system to prioritize patient choice and affordability. This includes promoting health savings accounts, expanding access to telemedicine, and encouraging competition among healthcare providers.

   - o **Reducing Costs**: Implementing measures to reduce the overall cost of healthcare, including negotiating drug prices and reducing administrative overhead.

4. **Education and Workforce Development**

   - o **School Choice**: Expanding school choice initiatives such as charter schools and voucher programs to provide parents with more options for their children's education.

   - o **Vocational Training**: Investing in vocational and technical education to equip workers with the skills needed for the modern economy, particularly in high-demand fields like technology and healthcare.

   - o **Curriculum Reform**: Advocating for a curriculum that emphasizes civic education, critical thinking, and STEM (Science, Technology, Engineering, and Mathematics) subjects.

5. **Energy Independence**

   - **Domestic Energy Production**: Promoting policies that support the development of domestic energy resources, including oil, natural gas, coal, and renewable energy sources.

   - **Innovation and Technology**: Encouraging innovation in energy technology to improve efficiency and reduce environmental impact while maintaining economic growth.

6. **Judicial and Legal Reforms**

   - **Judicial Appointments**: Appointing judges who adhere to a strict interpretation of the Constitution and uphold conservative principles.

   - **Legal Reforms**: Implementing legal reforms to protect individual liberties, reduce frivolous lawsuits, and ensure a fair and efficient judicial system.

7. **Immigration Reform**

   - **Legal Immigration**: Reforming the legal immigration system to prioritize skilled workers and ensure that immigrants contribute positively to the U.S. economy.

   - **Illegal Immigration**: Implementing strict measures to prevent illegal immigration, including enhanced border security and stricter enforcement of immigration laws.

8. **Infrastructure Development**

   - **Modernizing Infrastructure**: Investing in the modernization of America's infrastructure, including roads, bridges, airports, and public transportation systems.

- o **Private-Public Partnerships**: Encouraging private sector investment in infrastructure projects through public-private partnerships.

Implementation Strategy

Agenda 47 outlines a detailed strategy for implementing these policies, focusing on several key areas:

1. **Legislative Action**: Working with Congress to pass legislation that supports the objectives of Agenda 47. This includes building coalitions, lobbying efforts, and public advocacy.

2. **Executive Orders**: Utilizing executive orders to enact policy changes that do not require congressional approval. This allows for swift implementation of key initiatives.

3. **Public Engagement**: Engaging with the American public to build support for the policies outlined in Agenda 47. This includes grassroots organizing, media campaigns, and community outreach.

4. **Monitoring and Evaluation**: Continuously monitoring the progress of policy implementation and evaluating the impact of these policies. This ensures accountability and allows for adjustments as needed.

Challenges and Criticisms

Agenda 47 is not without its challenges and criticisms. Key issues include:

1. **Political Opposition**: Significant opposition from political adversaries who disagree with the policies and principles outlined in Agenda 47.

2. **Economic Feasibility**: Concerns about the economic feasibility of some proposed policies, particularly in terms of budget deficits and long-term fiscal sustainability.

3. **Public Perception**: Managing public perception and countering misinformation to ensure widespread support for the agenda.

Future Outlook

Agenda 47 represents a comprehensive and ambitious plan to shape America's future through conservative governance. By focusing on economic revival, national security, healthcare reform, education, energy independence, judicial reforms, immigration, and infrastructure, the agenda aims to restore American greatness and ensure long-term prosperity and security. The success of Agenda 47 depends on the collaborative efforts of policymakers, leaders, and the American public to achieve these transformative goals.

Importance of Conservative and Right-Wing Policies

Conservative and right-wing policies are foundational principles that emphasize limited government, free-market capitalism, individual liberties, traditional values, and a strong national defense. These policies have shaped significant aspects of American society and governance, advocating for personal responsibility, economic freedom, and a commitment to preserving the nation's cultural and moral fabric.

Core Principles of Conservative and Right-Wing Policies

1. **Limited Government**

   o **Federalism**: Conservatives advocate for a smaller federal government with more power vested in state and local governments. This decentralization allows for more tailored and responsive governance that reflects the unique needs of diverse communities.

- o **Fiscal Responsibility**: Emphasis on balanced budgets, reduced government spending, and minimizing public debt to ensure long-term economic stability and prevent burdens on future generations.

- o **Regulation Reduction**: Streamlining regulations to reduce bureaucratic red tape, thus fostering an environment where businesses can thrive and innovate without excessive government interference.

2. **Free-Market Capitalism**

- o **Economic Freedom**: Advocating for policies that promote entrepreneurship, competition, and innovation, allowing individuals and businesses to operate with minimal government intervention.

- o **Tax Policy**: Supporting lower tax rates to stimulate economic growth, investment, and job creation. The belief is that individuals and businesses are better stewards of their own resources than the government.

- o **Property Rights**: Ensuring strong protections for private property, which is seen as a cornerstone of economic freedom and prosperity.

3. **Individual Liberties**

- o **Personal Responsibility**: Encouraging individuals to take responsibility for their own lives and decisions, promoting self-reliance and independence.

- o **Freedom of Speech**: Defending the First Amendment rights, ensuring that individuals can express their views without fear of censorship or retaliation.

- ○ **Second Amendment Rights**: Upholding the right to bear arms as a means of personal protection and a safeguard against tyranny.

4. **Traditional Values**

   - ○ **Family and Community**: Placing a strong emphasis on the importance of family and community as the fundamental units of society. Policies often aim to strengthen these institutions through support for marriage, parenting, and local community initiatives.

   - ○ **Moral and Cultural Conservatism**: Advocating for policies that reflect traditional moral and cultural values, often rooted in religious beliefs and historical norms.

5. **Strong National Defense**

   - ○ **Military Strength**: Ensuring a robust and well-funded military to protect national interests, deter adversaries, and maintain global stability.

   - ○ **National Security**: Implementing policies that secure the nation's borders, enhance cybersecurity, and address emerging threats from state and non-state actors.

   - ○ **Foreign Policy**: Pursuing a foreign policy that prioritizes American interests, promotes global stability, and supports allies while being cautious about entanglement in prolonged conflicts.

Impact of Conservative and Right-Wing Policies

1. **Economic Growth and Stability**

   - ○ **Job Creation**: Lower taxes and deregulation often lead to increased business investment and job creation. Historical examples include the economic booms following the Reagan tax cuts in the 1980s and the Trump tax cuts in 2017.

- o **Innovation and Entrepreneurship**: A free-market environment encourages innovation and entrepreneurship, leading to technological advancements and new industries.

- o **Global Competitiveness**: Policies that foster economic freedom and reduce regulatory burdens can enhance the global competitiveness of American businesses.

2. **Social Cohesion and Stability**

- o **Strengthening Families**: Policies that support traditional family structures and community values can contribute to social stability and cohesion.

- o **Crime Reduction**: Strong support for law enforcement and criminal justice reforms focused on deterrence and rehabilitation can lead to lower crime rates and safer communities.

3. **Preservation of Individual Freedoms**

- o **Civil Liberties**: By emphasizing the protection of individual rights, conservative policies help preserve civil liberties and personal freedoms against potential government overreach.

- o **Religious Freedom**: Defending the right to practice one's religion without government interference is a cornerstone of conservative policy, reflecting the broader commitment to individual liberty.

4. **National Security and Global Leadership**

- o **Deterrence and Defense**: A strong military and robust national defense policies help deter potential adversaries and protect American interests worldwide.

- o **Global Stability**: Conservative foreign policy often seeks to promote global stability through strength and strategic alliances, contributing to a more secure international environment.

Criticisms and Challenges

1. **Economic Inequality**: Critics argue that conservative economic policies can lead to increased income inequality and insufficient support for the disadvantaged.

2. **Environmental Concerns**: Deregulation efforts, particularly in the energy sector, may lead to environmental degradation and insufficient action on climate change.

3. **Social Issues**: Policies rooted in traditional values may be seen as exclusionary or outdated by some segments of the population, particularly in relation to LGBTQ+ rights and reproductive freedoms.

4. **Government Efficiency**: The push for limited government and reduced public spending may result in underfunded public services and infrastructure, impacting overall quality of life.

Conservative and right-wing policies play a crucial role in shaping the political, economic, and social landscape of the United States. By emphasizing limited government, economic freedom, individual liberties, traditional values, and strong national defense, these policies aim to create a prosperous, free, and secure society. While they face criticisms and challenges, the principles underlying conservative and right-wing policies continue to influence American governance and public discourse, reflecting the enduring values of personal responsibility, freedom, and the rule of law.

Chapter 1 Historical Context

The Evolution of Conservative Policies in America

Conservative policies in America have undergone significant transformation since the nation's founding. Rooted in a commitment to limited government, individual liberty, and free-market principles, American conservatism has adapted to changing political, economic, and social landscapes over the centuries. This evolution reflects the interplay between foundational ideals and contemporary challenges, shaping the direction of the conservative movement and its influence on American governance.

Foundations of American Conservatism

1. **Early American Conservatism (18th and 19th Centuries)**

   o **Founding Principles**: The foundations of American conservatism can be traced back to the principles enshrined in the U.S. Constitution, emphasizing limited government, checks and balances, and the protection of individual rights. Influential figures like Alexander Hamilton and John Adams advocated for a strong but limited central government and a balanced approach to economic policy.

   o **Federalism**: Early American conservatism was characterized by a commitment to federalism, the division of power between the federal government and the states. This principle aimed to prevent the concentration of power and preserve the autonomy of states.

2. **Civil War and Reconstruction Era (Mid-19th Century)**

   o **States' Rights**: The Civil War and Reconstruction era highlighted tensions between federal authority and states' rights. Southern conservatives emphasized states' rights and limited federal intervention, particularly concerning issues like slavery and economic regulation.

- ○ **Reconstruction Policies**: Post-Civil War, conservative opposition to Reconstruction policies aimed at integrating formerly enslaved people into society and ensuring their civil rights, reflecting a preference for local control over federal mandates.

Progressive Era to New Deal (Late 19th to Early 20th Centuries)

1. **Response to Progressivism**

   - ○ **Economic Regulation**: The Progressive Era (1890s-1920s) introduced significant economic regulation and social reforms. Conservatives resisted these changes, advocating for laissez-faire economics and opposing government intervention in the marketplace.

   - ○ **Limited Government**: Conservative leaders like President William Howard Taft emphasized the importance of limited government and fiscal conservatism, opposing the expansion of federal power.

2. **The New Deal and Its Aftermath**

   - ○ **Opposition to New Deal Policies**: The Great Depression and Franklin D. Roosevelt's New Deal brought extensive government intervention in the economy. Conservatives like Herbert Hoover and Robert Taft opposed these policies, arguing that they undermined free-market principles and individual initiative.

   - ○ **Emergence of Modern Conservatism**: The New Deal era catalyzed the formation of modern American conservatism, which sought to defend free enterprise, limited government, and individual liberties against perceived encroachments by the federal government.

Post-World War II Conservatism (1940s-1970s)

1. **The Rise of the Conservative Movement**

   o **Intellectual Foundations**: The post-war period saw the emergence of influential conservative intellectuals like William F. Buckley Jr., who founded the National Review, and economist Milton Friedman. Their work laid the intellectual foundation for modern conservatism, emphasizing free-market economics, anti-communism, and traditional values.

   o **Cold War Conservatism**: Anti-communism became a central tenet of conservative policy during the Cold War, with leaders like Senator Joseph McCarthy and Barry Goldwater advocating for a strong national defense and aggressive stance against the Soviet Union.

2. **The Goldwater Campaign and Its Legacy**

   o **1964 Presidential Campaign**: Barry Goldwater's 1964 presidential campaign marked a pivotal moment in the conservative movement. Though he lost to Lyndon B. Johnson, Goldwater's candidacy galvanized conservative activists and laid the groundwork for future successes.

   o **Shaping the Republican Party**: Goldwater's emphasis on limited government, states' rights, and anti-communism reshaped the Republican Party, steering it towards a more conservative ideology.

The Reagan Revolution (1980s)

1. **Ronald Reagan's Presidency**

- o **Economic Policies**: Ronald Reagan's presidency (1981-1989) epitomized modern conservatism with his implementation of supply-side economics, tax cuts, deregulation, and a focus on reducing the size of government. Reaganomics aimed to spur economic growth through lower taxes and reduced government spending.

- o **Defense and Foreign Policy**: Reagan strengthened the U.S. military and adopted a robust anti-communist foreign policy, including the Strategic Defense Initiative (SDI) and support for anti-communist movements worldwide.

2. **Cultural Conservatism**

- o **Social Issues**: Reagan's era also saw a rise in cultural conservatism, with increased emphasis on traditional family values, opposition to abortion, and support for school prayer. This period solidified the alliance between conservative politics and the religious right.

Post-Reagan Conservatism (1990s-2000s)

1. **The Gingrich Revolution**

- o **Contract with America**: In the 1994 midterm elections, Newt Gingrich and the Republican Party introduced the "Contract with America," a legislative agenda focused on reducing government, welfare reform, and fiscal responsibility. The Republicans' subsequent electoral victory led to significant policy changes under President Bill Clinton's administration.

- o **Welfare Reform**: The 1996 welfare reform act, which aimed to reduce dependency on government assistance and encourage work, was a major conservative achievement during this period.

2. **George W. Bush's Presidency**

   - **Economic Policies**: George W. Bush's presidency (2001-2009) featured tax cuts, deregulation, and efforts to reform Social Security and Medicare. His administration's economic policies reflected traditional conservative priorities of reducing the tax burden and promoting free enterprise.

   - **War on Terror**: In response to the 9/11 attacks, Bush launched the War on Terror, significantly increasing defense spending and implementing policies aimed at protecting national security.

Contemporary Conservatism (2010s-Present)

1. **The Tea Party Movement**

   - **Grassroots Activism**: The Tea Party movement, emerging in 2009, epitomized grassroots conservative activism, focusing on reducing government spending, opposing tax increases, and advocating for constitutional adherence.

   - **Impact on Republican Politics**: The movement significantly influenced the Republican Party, pushing it further towards fiscal conservatism and limited government principles.

2. **Donald Trump's Presidency**

   - **Economic Nationalism**: Donald Trump's presidency (2017-2021) brought a blend of traditional conservatism and populist economic nationalism. Key policies included tax cuts, deregulation, and renegotiation of trade deals to favor American workers.

- o **Judicial Appointments**: Trump's appointment of conservative judges, including three Supreme Court justices, had a lasting impact on the judiciary, shaping American legal landscape for generations.

- o **Immigration and Border Security**: Trump emphasized strict immigration policies and enhanced border security, including the construction of a border wall.

Challenges and Future Directions

1. **Internal Divisions**: The conservative movement faces internal divisions between traditional conservatives, libertarians, and populists. Balancing these factions while maintaining a cohesive policy agenda is an ongoing challenge.

2. **Adaptation to Social Change**: Addressing evolving social issues, such as LGBTQ+ rights, racial justice, and technology regulation, requires conservatives to adapt their policies while adhering to core principles.

3. **Globalization and Economic Policy**: Navigating the complexities of globalization, trade, and economic inequality presents a significant challenge for contemporary conservative policymakers.

The evolution of conservative policies in America reflects a dynamic interplay between foundational principles and contemporary challenges. From the early days of the Republic to the present, conservatism has adapted to changing political, economic, and social landscapes while maintaining a commitment to limited government, individual liberty, free-market capitalism, and traditional values. As the conservative movement continues to evolve, it faces the task of addressing new challenges while preserving the core principles that have defined it for centuries.

Key Milestones Leading to Project 2025

Project 2025 represents a forward-looking initiative by the Heritage Foundation, aiming to shape conservative policy priorities and prepare America for future challenges and opportunities. The milestones leading to Project 2025 underscore the evolution of conservative thought and the strategic planning necessary to advance these principles in a rapidly changing world.

Early Foundations of Conservative Thought

1. **Founding of the Heritage Foundation (1973)**

   o The Heritage Foundation, established in 1973, emerged as a prominent conservative think tank dedicated to developing and promoting policy solutions grounded in free enterprise, limited government, individual freedom, traditional American values, and a strong national defense.

   o **Policy Development**: From its inception, Heritage focused on conducting rigorous research and analysis to influence public policy debates, laying the groundwork for future initiatives like Project 2025.

2. **Reagan Revolution (1980s)**

   o The presidency of Ronald Reagan in the 1980s marked a pivotal moment for conservative policies in America. Reagan's commitment to lower taxes, deregulation, and a strong national defense reshaped the political landscape and galvanized conservative principles.

   o **Policy Impact**: Reaganomics, characterized by supply-side economics and a focus on reducing government intervention in the economy, laid the economic foundation that would influence conservative policy development for decades.

Shifts in Conservative Strategy and Policy

1. **Contract with America (1994)**

   o The Contract with America, introduced by House Republicans led by Newt Gingrich in 1994, outlined a legislative agenda focused on fiscal responsibility, welfare reform, and limited government.

   o **Legislative Agenda**: This milestone demonstrated a unified approach among conservatives to advance specific policy goals, highlighting the importance of strategic planning and public engagement in shaping policy outcomes.

2. **Tea Party Movement (2009)**

   o Emerging in response to concerns over government spending and fiscal policy, the Tea Party movement became a grassroots force advocating for lower taxes, reduced government debt, and adherence to constitutional principles.

   o **Grassroots Activism**: The movement's influence on conservative policy emphasized the role of grassroots activism in shaping political discourse and policy priorities leading up to Project 2025.

Emergence of Project 2025

1. **Policy Innovation and Strategic Planning**

- o **Strategic Vision**: Project 2025 represents a strategic initiative by the Heritage Foundation to anticipate future policy challenges and opportunities facing America.

- o **Research and Analysis**: Leveraging decades of research and policy expertise, Project 2025 aims to develop innovative solutions that align with conservative principles while addressing contemporary issues such as economic growth, national security, healthcare reform, and technological advancements.

2. **Public Policy Debates and Influence**

- o **Thought Leadership**: Building on Heritage's legacy of thought leadership, Project 2025 seeks to influence public policy debates and shape the agenda for conservative governance.

- o **Policy Impact**: By outlining clear policy recommendations and advocating for their adoption, Project 2025 aims to guide policymakers and stakeholders in implementing reforms that promote economic prosperity, individual liberty, and national resilience.

Challenges and Future Directions

1. **Adaptation to Changing Dynamics**

- o **Globalization and Technology**: Addressing the impact of globalization, technological innovation, and demographic shifts requires Project 2025 to adapt conservative principles to new realities while maintaining core values.

- o **Policy Implementation**: Overcoming partisan divisions and ensuring the effective implementation of Project 2025's recommendations present ongoing challenges for conservative policymakers and advocates.

The milestones leading to Project 2025 reflect the evolution of conservative thought and strategy in America, from foundational principles to strategic initiatives aimed at shaping future policy directions. By building on historical achievements, responding to contemporary challenges, and anticipating future trends, Project 2025 underscores the Heritage Foundation's commitment to advancing conservative ideals and ensuring America's continued prosperity and resilience in the years ahead.

Donald Trump's Presidency and the Genesis of Agenda 47

Donald Trump's presidency (2017-2021) marked a significant chapter in American politics, characterized by populist rhetoric, unconventional governance style, and a focus on challenging establishment norms. His administration introduced several policy initiatives and priorities, including the genesis of Agenda 47, which aimed to address key issues and reshape American governance in alignment with Trump's vision and priorities.

Campaign Promises and Policy Priorities

1. **America First Agenda**

   o **Economic Policies**: Trump campaigned on revitalizing American manufacturing, renegotiating trade deals, and implementing protectionist measures to prioritize American jobs and industries.

   o **Tax Reform**: His administration passed the Tax Cuts and Jobs Act of 2017, which aimed to stimulate economic growth through corporate tax cuts and adjustments to individual tax rates.

- o **Deregulation**: Trump pursued deregulatory efforts across various sectors, aiming to reduce bureaucratic hurdles and stimulate business investment and expansion.

2. **Immigration and Border Security**

- o **Border Wall**: A cornerstone of Trump's immigration policy was the construction of a border wall along the U.S.-Mexico border to curb illegal immigration and enhance national security.

- o **Travel Bans**: He implemented travel bans from several predominantly Muslim countries, citing national security concerns and the need for enhanced vetting procedures.

Genesis of Agenda 47

1. **Policy Framework and Objectives**

- o **National Security**: Agenda 47 encompassed initiatives aimed at bolstering national security, including strengthening military capabilities, enhancing cybersecurity measures, and modernizing defense infrastructure.

- o **Trade and Economic Policy**: Trump's agenda prioritized fair trade deals and reducing trade deficits, often through bilateral negotiations and tariffs aimed at protecting American industries.

- o **Healthcare Reform**: Efforts to repeal and replace the Affordable Care Act (ACA) were central to Agenda 47, emphasizing market-based solutions and state flexibility in healthcare delivery.

2. **Judicial Appointments and Constitutional Conservatism**

- o **Supreme Court Nominations**: Trump appointed three Supreme Court justices, shifting the court's balance toward a more conservative interpretation of the Constitution.

- o **Federal Judiciary**: Beyond the Supreme Court, his administration prioritized appointing conservative judges to lower federal courts, aiming to influence legal precedents for years to come.

Challenges and Controversies

1. **Political Divisions and Legislative Challenges**

   - o **Partisan Gridlock**: Trump faced significant opposition from congressional Democrats, leading to legislative gridlock on key policy priorities such as healthcare reform and immigration.

   - o **Impeachment**: He was impeached twice by the House of Representatives, first on charges related to his interactions with Ukraine and second for his role in the January 6th Capitol riot.

2. **Public Perception and Media Relations**

   - o **Media Coverage**: Trump's presidency was characterized by strained relations with mainstream media outlets, with accusations of misinformation and bias shaping public perception of his administration.

   - o **Populist Appeal**: Despite controversies, Trump maintained a strong base of support among voters drawn to his outsider persona and promises to challenge the political establishment.

Legacy and Future Influence

1. **Impact on Republican Party and Conservative Movement**

- **Populist Shift**: Trump's presidency catalyzed a populist shift within the Republican Party, influencing its platform on trade, immigration, and foreign policy.

- **Continued Influence**: His endorsements of candidates and ongoing presence in political discourse continue to shape conservative policy debates and electoral dynamics.

Donald Trump's presidency left a lasting impact on American politics, policy, and governance. Through the genesis of Agenda 47 and other initiatives, his administration sought to reshape domestic and international priorities in line with his America First agenda. Despite facing significant challenges and controversies, Trump's presidency underscored the influence of populist rhetoric and unconventional leadership styles on contemporary American conservatism and political discourse. His legacy continues to shape the trajectory of the Republican Party and conservative movement as they navigate future electoral cycles and policy debates.

Chapter 2   Project 2025 Goals and Vision
Key Objectives of Project 2025

P roject 2025 represents a strategic initiative by the Heritage Foundation aimed at shaping conservative policy priorities and preparing America for future challenges and opportunities. The key objectives of Project 2025 encompass a broad range of policy areas, reflecting a comprehensive approach to advancing conservative principles and addressing pressing national issues.

Economic Growth and Fiscal Responsibility

1. **Promoting Economic Growth**

   o Project 2025 emphasizes policies that stimulate economic growth through tax reform, deregulation, and investment in innovation and infrastructure.

   o **Tax Policy**: Advocating for pro-growth tax policies that reduce burdens on businesses and individuals, encouraging entrepreneurship, job creation, and increased wages.

   o **Deregulation**: Removing regulatory barriers that stifle economic expansion and innovation, fostering a competitive business environment conducive to long-term growth.

2. **Ensuring Fiscal Responsibility**

   o Prioritizing fiscal discipline and responsible budgeting to reduce government spending, lower deficits, and address long-term fiscal challenges.

- o **Entitlement Reform**: Addressing unsustainable growth in entitlement programs to ensure their viability while promoting personal responsibility and fiscal sustainability.

National Security and Defense

1. Strengthening National Defense

- o Enhancing America's military capabilities and readiness to deter threats and protect national interests at home and abroad.

- o **Defense Modernization**: Investing in advanced defense technologies, cybersecurity capabilities, and modernizing military infrastructure to maintain strategic superiority.

2. Border Security and Immigration

- o Securing America's borders through enhanced border security measures, including physical barriers, advanced surveillance technologies, and robust enforcement of immigration laws.

- o **Immigration Reform**: Implementing merit-based immigration policies that prioritize skills, education, and contributions to the U.S. economy, while addressing illegal immigration challenges.

Healthcare Reform and Social Policy

1. Healthcare Innovation and Accessibility

- o Promoting market-based solutions to lower healthcare costs, expand access to quality care, and empower patients with choice and transparency.

- o **Repealing and Replacing Obamacare**: Advocating for alternatives to the Affordable Care Act (ACA) that increase competition among insurers, reduce premiums, and protect patient choice.

2. **Social Policy and Family Values**

- o Upholding traditional family values and promoting policies that support strong families, parental rights, and community-based solutions to social challenges.

- o **Education Reform**: Advancing school choice initiatives, empowering parents with educational options that best meet their children's needs and aspirations.

Energy Independence and Environmental Stewardship

1. **Achieving Energy Independence**

- o Developing America's energy resources responsibly to achieve energy independence, reduce reliance on foreign energy sources, and enhance national security.

- o **Energy Innovation**: Investing in clean energy technologies and promoting an "all-of-the-above" energy strategy that includes fossil fuels, renewables, and nuclear power.

2. **Environmental Conservation**

- o Balancing environmental conservation with economic growth by promoting market-based approaches, voluntary conservation efforts, and respecting property rights.

- Climate Policy: Rejecting one-size-fits-all climate regulations and supporting realistic approaches that prioritize American jobs and economic competitiveness.

Constitutional Governance and Judicial Reform

1. **Preserving Constitutional Principles**

   - Defending the Constitution's original intent, promoting federalism, and limiting government overreach into states' rights and individual liberties.

   - **Judicial Appointments**: Supporting judicial nominees who interpret the Constitution according to its original meaning and uphold the rule of law.

2. **Government Accountability and Transparency**

   - Promoting transparency in government operations, reducing bureaucratic inefficiencies, and holding elected officials accountable to taxpayers.

   - **Ethics Reform**: Implementing ethics reforms to restore public trust in government institutions and ensure integrity in public service.

The key objectives of Project 2025 reflect a comprehensive conservative agenda aimed at advancing economic prosperity, strengthening national security, promoting individual liberty, and preserving America's founding principles. By addressing critical policy areas through innovative solutions and principled leadership, Project 2025 seeks to secure America's future as a prosperous, free, and resilient nation.

Policy Framework and Strategic Initiatives

A robust policy framework forms the backbone of any strategic initiative, providing a structured approach to addressing complex challenges and achieving long-term objectives. This section delves into the components and strategic initiatives encompassed within a comprehensive policy framework, highlighting key principles and methodologies for effective governance and policy implementation.

Foundational Principles

1. **Conservative Values and Principles**

   o **Limited Government**: Emphasizing the role of government in protecting individual rights and liberties while minimizing regulatory interference in the private sector.

   o **Free Enterprise**: Promoting market-based solutions that encourage entrepreneurship, innovation, and economic growth without undue government intervention.

   o **Individual Freedom**: Safeguarding individual freedoms, including freedom of speech, religion, and association, as fundamental to a free and prosperous society.

2. **Constitutional Governance**

   o **Rule of Law**: Upholding the Constitution as the supreme law of the land, ensuring equal justice under law and protecting the rights of citizens from government overreach.

- **Separation of Powers**: Maintaining checks and balances among the executive, legislative, and judicial branches to prevent concentration of power and safeguard democratic principles.

Strategic Initiatives

1. **Economic Policy and Growth**

   - **Tax Reform**: Implementing pro-growth tax policies that stimulate investment, job creation, and economic expansion while ensuring fairness and simplicity in the tax code.

   - **Regulatory Reform**: Streamlining regulations to reduce bureaucratic burdens on businesses, promote innovation, and enhance competitiveness in the global marketplace.

   - **Trade Policy**: Negotiating fair and reciprocal trade agreements that protect American workers and industries while promoting free and fair trade practices globally.

2. **National Security and Defense**

   - **Defense Modernization**: Investing in advanced military technologies, infrastructure, and personnel to maintain military superiority and address emerging threats to national security.

   - **Cybersecurity**: Strengthening defenses against cyber threats, protecting critical infrastructure, and enhancing collaboration with international partners on cybersecurity initiatives.

- o **Border Security**: Securing borders through strategic investments in physical barriers, surveillance technologies, and comprehensive immigration reforms to enforce immigration laws effectively.

3. **Healthcare and Social Policy**

- o **Healthcare Reform**: Advancing patient-centered healthcare reforms that lower costs, expand access to quality care, and empower consumers with choices in healthcare coverage.

- o **Social Safety Net**: Strengthening social safety net programs to provide a safety net for those in need while promoting self-sufficiency and reducing dependency on government assistance.

- o **Education**: Promoting school choice initiatives, empowering parents with options for their children's education, and fostering innovation in educational practices to improve student outcomes.

4. **Energy Independence and Environmental Stewardship**

- o **Energy Policy**: Developing a comprehensive energy strategy that promotes energy independence, explores domestic energy resources, and supports clean energy innovation.

- o **Environmental Conservation**: Balancing environmental conservation with economic growth through market-based approaches, voluntary conservation efforts, and responsible stewardship of natural resources.

5. **Judicial Reform and Constitutional Governance**

- o **Judicial Appointments**: Nominating judges who interpret the Constitution according to its original meaning, uphold the rule of law, and respect judicial precedent.

- o **Government Accountability**: Enhancing transparency and accountability in government operations, reducing bureaucratic inefficiencies, and promoting ethical standards in public service.

- o **Federalism**: Defending states' rights and local governance autonomy, empowering states to address unique challenges and promote effective policy solutions at the local level.

A comprehensive policy framework and strategic initiatives are essential for achieving sustainable economic growth, enhancing national security, promoting individual liberty, and preserving constitutional principles. By adhering to conservative values and principles while implementing innovative policy solutions, policymakers can navigate complex challenges and chart a course toward a prosperous and resilient future for America. This framework ensures that governance is guided by principles of limited government, free enterprise, and individual freedom, fostering a society where opportunity thrives and individual potential is unleashed.

Expected Impact on Domestic Policy
Economic Growth and Prosperity

1. **Stimulating Economic Growth**

   - o Through tax reforms and deregulation, the policy framework aims to bolster economic growth by reducing barriers to business expansion, fostering innovation, and encouraging job creation.

   - o **Impact**: This could lead to increased GDP growth, higher wages, and improved living standards for Americans.

2. **Healthcare and Social Welfare**

o Reforming healthcare to lower costs and increase accessibility through market-based solutions and empowering individuals with healthcare choices.

o **Impact**: Improved healthcare outcomes, reduced healthcare spending, and a more efficient healthcare system benefiting American families.

3. **Education Reform**

o Promoting school choice and educational innovation to empower parents and improve educational outcomes for students across the country.

o **Impact**: Enhanced educational opportunities, improved academic performance, and workforce readiness.

4. **Energy Independence and Environmental Policy**

o Developing a comprehensive energy strategy to achieve energy independence, promote clean energy technologies, and balance environmental conservation with economic growth.

o **Impact**: Reduced dependence on foreign energy sources, job creation in the energy sector, and sustainable environmental practices.

5. **Judicial and Constitutional Reforms**

o Appointing judges who uphold constitutional principles, promote judicial restraint, and support federalism.

o **Impact**: Preservation of individual rights, protection of liberties, and a balanced approach to governance.

Expected Impact on Foreign Policy

National Security and Defense

1. **Enhancing Military Capabilities**

   ○ Modernizing defense infrastructure, investing in advanced technologies, and strengthening alliances to maintain global security leadership.

   ○ **Impact**: Deterrence of threats, enhanced national security posture, and safeguarding American interests abroad.

2. **Trade and Diplomacy**

   ○ Negotiating fair trade agreements, addressing trade imbalances, and promoting American exports.

   ○ **Impact**: Increased market access for American goods, job creation in export industries, and enhanced economic diplomacy.

3. **Immigration and Border Security**

   ○ Strengthening border security, enforcing immigration laws, and reforming immigration policies to prioritize national security and economic interests.

   ○ **Impact**: Reduced illegal immigration, improved border enforcement, and a more orderly immigration system.

4. **Cybersecurity and Global Challenges**

   ○ Addressing cybersecurity threats, promoting international cooperation on cyber defense, and countering global challenges such as terrorism and organized crime.

   ○ **Impact**: Enhanced resilience against cyber threats, strengthened international partnerships, and global stability.

5. **Human Rights and Global Leadership**

- o Championing human rights, promoting democracy, and advancing American values on the global stage.

- o **Impact**: Strengthened alliances, increased global influence, and support for democratic movements worldwide.

The expected impact on domestic and foreign policy under this strategic framework is poised to reshape America's role in the world and address critical domestic challenges. By focusing on economic growth, national security, healthcare reform, energy independence, judicial integrity, and global leadership, policymakers aim to foster prosperity at home while advancing American interests abroad. This approach underscores the importance of strategic planning, diplomatic engagement, and principled leadership in shaping a prosperous future for the United States and its citizens.

Chapter 4   Agenda 47 Trump's Vision
Core Principles of Agenda 47

Agenda 47 emerged as a strategic framework underpinning the policy priorities and initiatives championed by the Trump administration. It encapsulates core principles aimed at advancing a conservative agenda focused on revitalizing American governance, enhancing national security, promoting economic prosperity, and addressing key domestic challenges.

Foundational Principles

1. **America First**

   o **National Sovereignty**: Emphasizing the primacy of American interests in international relations, trade negotiations, and diplomatic engagements.

   o **Economic Patriotism**: Promoting policies that prioritize American workers, industries, and economic growth through fair trade practices and regulatory reforms.

2. **Conservative Values**

   o **Limited Government**: Advocating for reduced federal intervention in areas best managed by states and localities, fostering individual liberty and personal responsibility.

   o **Constitutional Governance**: Upholding the Constitution, including the protection of individual rights, the rule of law, and separation of powers.

Key Policy Priorities

1. **Economic Policy**

- o **Tax Reform**: Implementing tax cuts aimed at stimulating economic growth, incentivizing business investment, and fostering job creation.

- o **Regulatory Relief**: Rolling back excessive regulations perceived to stifle innovation, economic competitiveness, and entrepreneurship.

2. **National Security and Defense**

- o **Military Strength**: Prioritizing the modernization of military capabilities, enhancing defense infrastructure, and investing in advanced technologies to maintain military superiority.

- o **Border Security**: Implementing measures to secure U.S. borders, including the construction of physical barriers and enhancing border enforcement to curb illegal immigration.

3. **Trade and Diplomacy**

- o **Fair Trade**: Advocating for fair and reciprocal trade agreements that protect American interests, reduce trade deficits, and promote job growth in domestic industries.

- o **Diplomatic Engagement**: Conducting foreign policy guided by American interests, emphasizing bilateral relationships, and leveraging economic leverage in international negotiations.

4. **Immigration Reform**

- o **Merit-Based Immigration**: Supporting immigration policies that prioritize skills, education, and merit-based criteria to meet economic and national security needs.

- Enforcement: Strengthening immigration enforcement measures to address illegal immigration and ensure compliance with U.S. immigration laws.

5. **Healthcare and Social Policy**

   - **Healthcare Reform**: Pursuing alternatives to the Affordable Care Act (ACA) aimed at reducing healthcare costs, expanding consumer choice, and improving healthcare outcomes.

   - **Social Safety Net**: Promoting reforms to welfare programs to encourage self-sufficiency, reduce dependency, and streamline government assistance.

Impact and Legacy

Agenda 47 reflects a commitment to advancing conservative principles and policies aimed at reshaping domestic governance and reinforcing America's global standing. By prioritizing economic growth, national security, constitutional governance, and American interests in international affairs, Agenda 47 sought to fulfill campaign promises and address longstanding challenges facing the nation. Its implementation and subsequent impact continue to shape political discourse and policy debates within the conservative movement and beyond.

The core principles of Agenda 47 underscore its commitment to advancing a conservative agenda centered on America First policies, economic revitalization, national security, and constitutional governance. By aligning policy priorities with these principles, the Trump administration aimed to redefine government priorities, enhance American competitiveness, and safeguard the interests of the American people both at home and abroad.

Economic Policies and Reforms

Economic policies play a pivotal role in shaping a nation's economic landscape, influencing growth, employment, and overall prosperity. This section delves into the comprehensive economic policies and reforms aimed at stimulating economic growth, enhancing competitiveness, and fostering a favorable business environment.

Tax Policy

1. **Tax Cuts and Jobs Act (TCJA)**

   o Implemented in 2017, TCJA aimed to simplify the tax code, lower tax rates for individuals and businesses, and incentivize investment.

   o **Impact**: Reduced corporate tax rate from 35% to 21%, leading to increased business investment, job creation, and economic expansion.

2. **Individual Income Taxes**

   o Adjusted tax brackets and reduced marginal tax rates for individuals, providing relief for middle-class taxpayers.

   o **Impact**: Higher disposable income, increased consumer spending, and economic stimulus.

3. **Capital Investment**

   o Introduced provisions allowing for immediate expensing of capital investments, encouraging businesses to invest in equipment and infrastructure.

   o **Impact**: Boosted capital expenditures, modernized infrastructure, and enhanced productivity.

Regulatory Reform

1. **Deregulation**

   - Rolled back regulations perceived as burdensome to businesses, particularly in industries like energy, finance, and healthcare.

   - **Impact**: Reduced compliance costs, increased business confidence, and facilitated innovation and entrepreneurship.

2. **Financial Sector Reform**

   - Reformed Dodd-Frank Wall Street Reform and Consumer Protection Act to ease regulatory requirements on small and medium-sized banks.

   - **Impact**: Enhanced access to capital for businesses, improved lending conditions, and supported community banks.

Trade Policy

1. **Trade Agreements**

   - Negotiated new trade agreements and revised existing ones to promote fair and reciprocal trade practices.

   - **Impact**: Increased market access for American goods and services, reduced trade deficits, and protected intellectual property rights.

2. **Tariffs and Trade Relations**

   - Implemented tariffs on imported goods, particularly from China, to address trade imbalances and protect domestic industries.

   - **Impact**: Controversy over effects on consumer prices, retaliatory tariffs from trading partners, and negotiations for trade resolution.

Labor Market Policies

1. **Workforce Development**

   o Promoted apprenticeships and vocational training programs to equip workers with skills aligned with industry demands.

   o **Impact**: Reduced unemployment, improved labor force participation, and bridged skills gap in key sectors.

2. **Minimum Wage and Labor Standards**

   o Supported state-level initiatives for minimum wage adjustments and maintained federal labor standards.

   o **Impact**: Varied impacts across states, debates over economic implications, and balancing wage growth with business viability.

Infrastructure Investment

1. **Infrastructure Plan**

   o Proposed infrastructure investment plan to modernize roads, bridges, airports, and other critical infrastructure.

   o **Impact**: Job creation in construction and related sectors, improved infrastructure quality, and enhanced economic efficiency.

Monetary Policy

1. **Federal Reserve**

   o Coordinated monetary policy to maintain stable prices, maximize employment, and support economic growth.

   o **Impact**: Interest rate adjustments, inflation control, and financial market stability.

The economic policies and reforms implemented aimed to stimulate economic growth, enhance competitiveness, and foster a favorable business environment. By addressing tax reform, deregulation, trade policy, labor market initiatives, infrastructure investment, and monetary policy, policymakers sought to create conditions conducive to sustainable economic expansion, job creation, and prosperity for all Americans. These policies continue to shape economic debates and policy discussions, reflecting efforts to balance growth with fiscal responsibility and ensure long-term economic resilience.

Foreign Policy and National Security

Foreign policy and national security are integral components of a nation's governance, shaping international relations, safeguarding sovereignty, and promoting global stability. This section explores the multifaceted aspects of U.S. foreign policy and national security strategies, encompassing diplomatic engagements, military alliances, economic interests, and geopolitical priorities.

Diplomatic Engagement

1. **Bilateral and Multilateral Relations**

   o Strengthening alliances with key partners, including NATO allies, Asian-Pacific countries, and regional coalitions to promote shared security interests.

   o **Impact**: Enhanced diplomatic ties, collaborative efforts on global challenges, and strategic cooperation in counterterrorism and peacekeeping missions.

2. Diplomatic Initiatives

- o Advancing diplomatic initiatives to resolve conflicts, facilitate peace negotiations, and promote human rights and democracy worldwide.

- o **Impact**: Diplomatic achievements, mediation efforts in regional disputes, and support for international organizations promoting global governance.

Military Strategy and Defense

1. Military Readiness and Modernization

- o Modernizing military capabilities, investing in advanced technologies, and maintaining readiness to deter adversaries and respond to emerging threats.

- o **Impact**: Enhanced defense capabilities, rapid response to crises, and preservation of military superiority.

2. Counterterrorism and Homeland Security

- o Combating terrorism through international partnerships, intelligence sharing, and military operations targeting terrorist organizations and their networks.

- o **Impact**: Disruption of terrorist activities, safeguarding homeland security, and preventing terrorist attacks on U.S. soil and abroad.

Economic Interests and Trade Relations

1. Trade Agreements and Economic Diplomacy

- Negotiating trade agreements to expand market access for American goods and services, promote economic growth, and address trade imbalances.

- **Impact**: Economic benefits, job creation in export industries, and strengthening of economic ties with strategic partners.

2. **Sanctions and Economic Measures**

- Imposing sanctions on countries or entities violating international norms, human rights abuses, or engaging in illicit activities detrimental to global security.

- **Impact**: Economic pressure on targeted entities, diplomatic leverage in negotiations, and enforcement of international laws and regulations.

Geopolitical Strategy and Regional Focus

1. **Regional Stability and Conflict Resolution**

- Addressing regional conflicts, supporting peace initiatives, and providing humanitarian aid to stabilize volatile regions.

- **Impact**: Promotion of stability, conflict resolution efforts, and humanitarian assistance to affected populations.

2. **Strategic Competition and Great Power Rivalry**

- Managing strategic competition with global powers, including China and Russia, through diplomatic engagements, economic strategies, and military deterrence.

- **Impact**: Mitigation of geopolitical tensions, preservation of global security architecture, and protection of U.S. interests in contested regions.

Cybersecurity and Emerging Threats

1. **Cyber Defense and Information Security**

   - Enhancing cybersecurity measures, defending against cyber threats, and promoting international norms for responsible cyberspace behavior.

   - **Impact**: Protection of critical infrastructure, safeguarding of digital assets, and resilience against cyber attacks.

Foreign policy and national security strategies are crucial for safeguarding America's interests, promoting global stability, and upholding international norms. By integrating diplomatic engagements, military readiness, economic diplomacy, and cybersecurity measures, policymakers aim to navigate complex geopolitical challenges, advance U.S. leadership on the world stage, and ensure the security and prosperity of the United States and its allies. These strategies reflect a commitment to strategic alliances, global cooperation, and the pursuit of peace and stability in an increasingly interconnected world.

Chapter 5 Synergies Between Project 2025 and Agenda 47
Common Goals and Objectives

P roject 2025 and Agenda 47 represent strategic frameworks aimed at advancing conservative policies and reforming governance in the United States. This section explores the synergies between these initiatives, highlighting their shared objectives, policy priorities, and the overarching vision for America's future.

Introduction

Project 2025, developed by the Heritage Foundation, outlines a comprehensive agenda focusing on economic prosperity, national security, constitutional governance, and American leadership. Agenda 47, championed during Donald Trump's presidency, reflects a commitment to America First policies, economic revitalization, and strengthening national sovereignty. Together, these frameworks converge on several key areas, leveraging synergies to achieve transformative outcomes.

Economic Policies and Growth

1. **Tax Reform and Economic Stimulus**

   - **Project 2025**: Advocates for tax cuts, regulatory relief, and incentives to spur business investment and job creation.

   - **Agenda 47**: Implemented the Tax Cuts and Jobs Act (TCJA), reducing corporate taxes and promoting economic growth through deregulation and fiscal incentives.

o **Synergy**: Both initiatives prioritize economic policies that reduce government intervention, stimulate entrepreneurship, and foster a competitive business environment.

2. **Trade and Economic Diplomacy**

   o **Project 2025**: Emphasizes fair trade agreements, reducing trade deficits, and promoting American exports.

   o **Agenda 47**: Negotiates trade deals that prioritize American interests, enforce trade agreements, and protect intellectual property rights.

   o **Synergy**: Shared focus on economic diplomacy to enhance market access, support domestic industries, and advance economic interests globally.

National Security and Defense

1. **Military Modernization and Readiness**

   o **Project 2025**: Calls for robust defense spending, modernizing military capabilities, and enhancing national security preparedness.

   o **Agenda 47**: Prioritizes military strength, border security, and combating global terrorism through enhanced defense capabilities.

   o **Synergy**: Mutual commitment to strengthening America's defense posture, modernizing military infrastructure, and safeguarding national interests against emerging threats.

2. **Cybersecurity and Homeland Security**

   o **Project 2025**: Focuses on cybersecurity initiatives to protect critical infrastructure and defend against cyber threats.

- o **Agenda 47**: Implements cybersecurity measures to secure digital assets, promote responsible cyber behavior, and ensure national resilience.

- o **Synergy**: Collaborative efforts to enhance cybersecurity frameworks, mitigate cyber risks, and safeguard America's technological infrastructure.

Constitutional Governance and Judicial Reform

1. **Judicial Appointments and Constitutional Integrity**

   - o **Project 2025**: Advocates for judicial appointments that uphold constitutional principles, protect individual liberties, and promote judicial restraint.

   - o **Agenda 47**: Prioritizes appointing judges who interpret the Constitution strictly, defend individual rights, and support federalism.

   - o **Synergy**: Shared commitment to judicial reform, ensuring a balanced judiciary that interprets laws based on constitutional fidelity and protects fundamental freedoms.

The synergies between Project 2025 and Agenda 47 underscore their alignment on key policy priorities, from economic revitalization and national security to constitutional governance and judicial reform. By leveraging shared objectives and complementary strategies, these initiatives aim to reshape governance, strengthen American leadership, and advance conservative principles that prioritize economic prosperity, national sovereignty, and individual freedoms. Their collaborative approach reflects a commitment to shaping a future where America remains resilient, competitive, and secure in an evolving global landscape.

Collaborative Strategies for Policy Implementation

Effective policy implementation requires collaborative efforts across multiple stakeholders, leveraging diverse expertise, resources, and public engagement. This section examines the key components and strategies essential for successful policy implementation:

1. Stakeholder Engagement and Consultation

- **Inclusive Approach**: Engage stakeholders early in the policy development process to gather insights, address concerns, and build consensus.

- **Public Participation**: Foster transparency and accountability through public consultations, hearings, and feedback mechanisms to ensure policies reflect community needs.

- **Partnership Building**: Form alliances with governmental agencies, non-profit organizations, academia, and private sector entities to pool resources and expertise.

2. Policy Design and Formulation

- **Evidence-Based Approach**: Base policy decisions on thorough research, data analysis, and impact assessments to predict outcomes and inform decision-making.

- **Clear Objectives and Targets**: Define specific goals, measurable targets, and timelines to guide policy implementation and evaluate effectiveness.

- **Flexibility and Adaptability**: Design policies with built-in flexibility to adapt to changing circumstances, unforeseen challenges, and emerging opportunities.

3. Resource Allocation and Budgeting

- **Financial Planning**: Allocate resources effectively to prioritize policy initiatives, address critical needs, and optimize budgetary allocations.

- **Cost-Benefit Analysis**: Conduct rigorous cost-benefit analyses to assess the economic feasibility, long-term sustainability, and return on investment of policy interventions.

- **Performance Metrics**: Establish performance indicators and benchmarks to monitor progress, measure impact, and ensure accountability.

4. Interagency Coordination and Collaboration

- **Cross-Agency Collaboration**: Foster interagency cooperation and coordination to streamline processes, eliminate duplication, and enhance service delivery.

- **Task Forces and Working Groups**: Establish task forces or working groups to address complex issues, facilitate information sharing, and promote collaborative problem-solving.

- **Leadership and Oversight**: Appoint leadership roles and establish oversight mechanisms to manage interagency initiatives, resolve conflicts, and ensure alignment with strategic priorities.

5. Monitoring, Evaluation, and Feedback Mechanisms

- **Continuous Monitoring**: Implement robust monitoring systems to track policy implementation progress, identify bottlenecks, and make timely adjustments.

- **Evaluation Framework**: Conduct periodic evaluations and reviews to assess policy outcomes, measure impact on target populations, and identify areas for improvement.

- **Feedback Loops**: Establish feedback loops to solicit input from stakeholders, gather lessons learned, and incorporate stakeholder feedback into policy refinements.

6. Communication and Public Awareness

- **Effective Communication Strategies**: Develop clear and concise communication plans to educate the public, raise awareness about policy objectives, and garner support.

- **Transparency and Accountability**: Communicate policy decisions, outcomes, and challenges transparently to build trust, manage expectations, and maintain accountability.

- **Crisis Communication**: Prepare contingency plans and communication strategies to address crises, manage public perception, and maintain stakeholder confidence.

Collaborative strategies for policy implementation are essential to navigate complexities, achieve policy goals, and deliver meaningful outcomes for stakeholders. By fostering inclusive stakeholder engagement, designing evidence-based policies, optimizing resource allocation, promoting interagency collaboration, and establishing robust monitoring mechanisms, policymakers can enhance governance effectiveness, build public trust, and drive sustainable development. These strategies underscore the importance of collaboration, transparency, and adaptive leadership in shaping policies that address societal challenges and contribute to long-term prosperity and well-being.

Strengthening America's Global Position

Strengthening America's global position involves a multifaceted approach encompassing diplomatic engagements, economic strategies, military alliances, and cultural influence. This section explores the comprehensive efforts aimed at bolstering America's leadership and influence on the world stage.

Diplomatic Engagements and Alliances

1. **Multilateral Diplomacy**

   o Engaging with international organizations like the United Nations, NATO, and regional alliances to promote shared values, global security, and cooperation on pressing issues.

   o **Impact**: Enhanced diplomatic relations, collaborative efforts on peacekeeping missions, and collective responses to global crises such as climate change and pandemics.

2. **Bilateral Relations**

   o Strengthening alliances with key partners and allies, including strategic dialogues, trade agreements, and joint initiatives in areas such as defense, technology, and health.

   o **Impact**: Strengthened security partnerships, increased economic cooperation, and mutual support in advancing common interests and regional stability.

Economic Leadership and Trade Policy

1. **Global Economic Engagement**

   o Promoting free and fair trade agreements, reducing trade barriers, and advocating for open markets to expand economic opportunities for American businesses and workers.

   o **Impact**: Increased market access, job creation, and economic growth through exports, foreign direct investment, and technological innovation.

2. **Innovation and Technology Leadership**

   o Leading advancements in technology, research, and development to maintain competitiveness in critical sectors such as artificial intelligence, biotechnology, and space exploration.

   o **Impact**: Pioneering breakthroughs, setting global standards, and driving technological advancements that benefit global industries and enhance national security.

Military Strength and Strategic Security

1. **Defense Preparedness**

   o Investing in defense capabilities, modernizing military infrastructure, and maintaining readiness to deter threats, protect allies, and uphold global security commitments.

   o **Impact**: Enhanced deterrence capabilities, rapid response to emerging threats, and strategic stability in regions critical to U.S. national interests.

2. **Counterterrorism and Cybersecurity**

- o Combating terrorism through international partnerships, intelligence sharing, and coordinated military operations to disrupt terrorist networks and prevent attacks.

- o **Impact**: Improved global security cooperation, reduced terrorist threats, and strengthened cybersecurity resilience against cyber attacks and digital threats.

Cultural Diplomacy and Soft Power

1. **Promotion of American Values**

   - o Showcasing American culture, education, and democratic principles through cultural exchanges, educational programs, and public diplomacy initiatives.

   - o **Impact**: Building mutual understanding, fostering goodwill, and promoting democratic ideals globally to counter authoritarian influences and promote global stability.

Humanitarian Leadership and Global Health

1. **Global Health Initiatives**

   - o Addressing global health challenges, pandemics, and public health emergencies through humanitarian aid, health diplomacy, and support for global health organizations.

   - o **Impact**: Saving lives, promoting health security, and strengthening America's reputation as a leader in global health governance and crisis response.

Strengthening America's global position requires a coordinated approach across diplomatic, economic, military, and cultural domains. By fostering robust alliances, advancing economic leadership, maintaining military readiness, promoting American values through cultural diplomacy, and addressing global challenges through humanitarian efforts, the United States can assert its leadership, influence global norms, and advance shared prosperity and security worldwide. These efforts underscore America's commitment to global leadership, collaboration with allies and partners, and safeguarding a stable, prosperous future for all nations.

Chapter 6 Economic Policies
Tax Reforms and Economic Growth

Tax reforms play a pivotal role in shaping economic growth by influencing business investment, consumer spending, and overall economic activity. This section explores various aspects of tax reforms, their objectives, implementation strategies, and their broader implications for economic prosperity.

1. Objectives of Tax Reforms

Tax reforms are typically aimed at achieving several key objectives:

- **Stimulating Economic Growth**: By reducing tax burdens on businesses and individuals, governments aim to incentivize investment, innovation, and entrepreneurial activity.

- **Enhancing Competitiveness**: Lowering corporate taxes and simplifying tax codes can improve the competitiveness of domestic businesses in the global market, attracting foreign investment and promoting exports.

- **Ensuring Fairness and Equity**: Reforms often seek to create a fairer tax system by closing loopholes, eliminating preferential treatment, and ensuring that all taxpayers contribute proportionately to public revenues.

- **Boosting Government Revenue**: While some reforms focus on tax cuts to stimulate growth, others aim to broaden the tax base or streamline collection mechanisms to increase overall revenue.

2. Types of Tax Reforms

Tax reforms can take various forms, each with its specific impact on economic growth:

- **Corporate Tax Cuts**: Lowering corporate tax rates encourages businesses to invest in expansion, research and development (R&D), and job creation, thereby stimulating economic growth.

- **Individual Income Tax Adjustments**: Adjusting income tax brackets, deductions, and credits can increase disposable income for consumers, boosting spending and aggregate demand.

- **Simplification and Streamlining**: Simplifying tax codes and reducing compliance burdens for businesses and individuals can lower administrative costs and encourage compliance.

- **Incentives for Investment**: Providing tax incentives for specific industries or activities (e.g., renewable energy, infrastructure) can spur targeted economic development and innovation.

3. Impact on Economic Growth

Tax reforms have a profound impact on economic growth through several channels:

- **Investment and Business Climate**: Lower corporate taxes incentivize capital investment, expansion, and job creation, fostering a more dynamic business environment.

- **Consumer Spending**: Adjustments in individual income taxes can increase disposable income, boosting consumer spending on goods and services.

- **Entrepreneurship and Innovation**: Tax incentives for startups and R&D encourage innovation and entrepreneurship, driving technological advancements and productivity gains.

- **International Competitiveness**: Competitive tax policies attract foreign direct investment (FDI) and promote exports, enhancing a country's position in the global economy.

4. Challenges and Considerations

Despite their potential benefits, tax reforms also pose challenges:

- **Budgetary Constraints**: Balancing tax cuts with revenue needs requires careful fiscal management to avoid budget deficits and ensure sustainability.

- **Distributional Effects**: Reforms may impact different income groups differently, raising concerns about income inequality and social equity.

- **Implementation and Compliance**: Effective implementation and enforcement are critical to realizing the intended benefits of tax reforms and minimizing unintended consequences.

5. Case Studies and Examples

- **Tax Cuts and Jobs Act (TCJA)**: Implemented in the United States in 2017, the TCJA reduced corporate tax rates and introduced various provisions aimed at stimulating economic growth and repatriating offshore profits.

- **Tax Reforms in Developing Economies**: Many developing countries implement tax reforms to attract investment, broaden the tax base, and improve revenue collection capacity.

Tax reforms are powerful policy tools that can significantly influence economic growth, investment dynamics, and international competitiveness. By aligning tax policies with economic objectives, promoting fairness and efficiency, and addressing implementation challenges, governments can foster sustainable economic development and improve standards of living for their citizens. Understanding the nuanced impacts of tax reforms is crucial for policymakers, economists, and businesses alike in navigating complex global economic landscapes.

Driving Economic Growth and Innovation

Deregulation and business incentives are critical policy measures aimed at fostering a favorable business environment, promoting economic growth, and encouraging innovation. This section delves into the various aspects of deregulation, its objectives, implementation strategies, and the broader implications for businesses and the economy.

1. Objectives of Deregulation

Deregulation refers to the process of reducing or eliminating government regulations and bureaucratic barriers that restrict business activities. The primary objectives of deregulation include:

- **Promoting Economic Efficiency**: Streamlining regulations can reduce compliance costs, bureaucratic inefficiencies, and market distortions, allowing businesses to operate more efficiently.

- **Encouraging Competition**: Removing entry barriers and restrictive regulations can foster competition, driving innovation, lowering prices, and improving consumer choice.

- **Stimulating Investment**: Creating a business-friendly environment attracts domestic and foreign investment, spurring job creation, infrastructure development, and economic growth.

- **Enhancing Regulatory Clarity**: Simplifying regulatory frameworks and enhancing transparency can provide businesses with clear guidelines, reducing uncertainty and promoting long-term planning.

2. Types of Deregulation

Deregulation can take various forms across different sectors of the economy:

- **Financial Deregulation**: Removing restrictions on financial institutions can facilitate access to capital, promote lending, and enhance financial market efficiency.

- **Labor Market Deregulation**: Reforming labor laws and regulations can increase labor market flexibility, reduce hiring costs, and promote employment growth.

- **Environmental Deregulation**: Streamlining environmental regulations while ensuring sustainable practices can lower compliance costs for businesses while maintaining environmental stewardship.

- **Sector-Specific Deregulation**: Targeted reforms in sectors such as telecommunications, energy, and transportation can promote competition, innovation, and infrastructure development.

3. Impact on Business and Economic Growth

Deregulation and business incentives have significant implications for business operations and economic outcomes:

- **Business Competitiveness**: Reduced regulatory burdens enable businesses to innovate, invest in technology, and improve productivity, enhancing their competitiveness in domestic and global markets.

- **Job Creation and Investment**: Deregulation can stimulate job creation by lowering barriers to business entry, encouraging entrepreneurship, and attracting investment in new ventures and industries.

- **Innovation and Entrepreneurship**: Streamlined regulations promote entrepreneurial activity and innovation by allowing businesses to experiment with new products, services, and business models.

- **Cost Reductions**: Lower compliance costs and administrative burdens free up resources that businesses can redirect toward expansion, research, and development.

4. Challenges and Considerations

Despite its potential benefits, deregulation poses challenges and considerations:

- **Risk of Market Failures**: Insufficient regulation can lead to market failures, such as monopolistic practices, environmental degradation, or inadequate consumer protection.

- **Social and Environmental Impact**: Balancing deregulation with social welfare and environmental sustainability requires careful consideration to mitigate negative externalities.

- **Regulatory Oversight**: Maintaining effective regulatory oversight and enforcement mechanisms are essential to prevent abuses, ensure fair competition, and protect public interests.

5. Case Studies and Examples

- **Telecommunications Deregulation**: Deregulation in the telecommunications sector has led to increased competition, expanded access to services, and technological advancements in mobile and broadband networks.

- **Energy Sector Deregulation**: Reforms in energy markets have encouraged investment in renewable energy sources, enhanced grid reliability, and provided consumers with more choices and lower prices.

Deregulation and business incentives are vital tools for fostering economic growth, enhancing business competitiveness, and promoting innovation. By removing regulatory barriers, streamlining administrative processes, and incentivizing investment, governments can create a conducive environment for businesses to thrive, create jobs, and contribute to sustainable economic development. However, careful planning, stakeholder engagement, and ongoing evaluation are crucial to ensure that deregulatory efforts achieve their intended objectives while safeguarding public interests and promoting inclusive growth.

Trade Policies and International Relations

In the frameworks of Project 2025 by the Heritage Foundation and Agenda 47 during Donald Trump's presidency, trade policies play a critical role in shaping international relations, economic strategies, and geopolitical dynamics.

1. Strategic Objectives and Goals

- **Project 2025 (Heritage Foundation)**:

  - **Promoting Free Trade**: Advocating for policies that reduce barriers to trade, enhance market access for American goods and services, and foster economic growth through international commerce.

  - **Negotiating Fair Trade Agreements**: Emphasizing bilateral and multilateral trade agreements that prioritize American interests, fair trade practices, and reciprocity in economic relationships.

- o **Economic Security**: Ensuring robust economic security through trade policies that protect critical industries, strengthen national supply chains, and safeguard against unfair trade practices.

- **Agenda 47 (Donald Trump)**:

  - o **America First Trade Policies**: Prioritizing American economic interests, reducing trade deficits, and renegotiating trade agreements to benefit American workers and industries.

  - o **Tariff Measures**: Implementing tariffs and trade barriers strategically to address perceived trade imbalances, protect domestic industries, and negotiate better trade terms with international partners.

  - o **Bilateral Trade Deals**: Focusing on bilateral trade negotiations to secure favorable terms, promote American exports, and strengthen economic ties with key allies and trading partners.

2. Implementation Strategies

- **Policy Alignment**: Ensuring trade policies under Project 2025 and Agenda 47 align with broader economic and national security strategies to enhance competitiveness and economic resilience.

- **Trade Negotiations**: Actively engaging in negotiations to reform international trade rules, enhance market access, and protect intellectual property rights, reflecting the priorities of both initiatives.

- **Geopolitical Considerations**: Integrating trade policies with geopolitical objectives to strengthen alliances, address global challenges, and advance U.S. influence in key regions.

3. Impact on International Relations

- **Diplomatic Relations**: Trade policies under Project 2025 and Agenda 47 serve as diplomatic tools to strengthen alliances, resolve disputes, and foster cooperation on shared economic and security priorities.

- **Global Economic Order**: Shaping the global economic order by promoting fair trade practices, reducing trade barriers, and advocating for rules-based trade agreements that benefit American interests.

- **Geopolitical Dynamics**: Influencing geopolitical dynamics through economic statecraft, leveraging trade negotiations to achieve strategic objectives and enhance U.S. leadership in global affairs.

4. Challenges and Considerations

- **Trade Disputes**: Managing potential trade disputes and retaliatory measures resulting from tariff policies and renegotiated trade agreements.

- **Economic Resilience**: Ensuring trade policies contribute to long-term economic resilience, job creation, and sustainable growth in key sectors of the economy.

- **Multilateral Engagement**: Balancing bilateral trade negotiations with multilateral engagement to uphold international norms, institutions, and cooperative frameworks.

5. Future Directions

- **Innovation and Technology**: Harnessing trade policies to foster innovation, technology exchange, and digital trade opportunities that drive economic competitiveness and technological leadership.

- **Global Leadership**: Strengthening America's global leadership role through proactive engagement in international trade forums, advocating for reforms, and advancing U.S. economic interests on the world stage.

Trade policies within Project 2025 (Heritage Foundation) and Agenda 47 (Donald Trump) are integral to advancing American economic interests, enhancing international relations, and shaping global economic dynamics. By strategically aligning trade policies with broader national security and economic objectives, these initiatives aim to bolster U.S. competitiveness, promote fair trade practices, and strengthen alliances while navigating the complexities of global trade relations.

Chapter 7   National Security and Defense
Military Strength and Modernization

1. Strategic Vision and Objectives

Project 2025

- **Ensuring Military Readiness**: Project 2025 emphasizes the importance of maintaining a highly trained and well-equipped military to meet current and future threats. This involves continuous investment in personnel, equipment, and training programs.

- **Modernizing Defense Capabilities**: Focuses on upgrading existing military technology and developing new capabilities to address emerging threats. This includes cyber warfare, space defense, and advanced weaponry.

- **Strategic Alliances and Partnerships**: Strengthens alliances with key global partners through joint military exercises, intelligence sharing, and defense agreements. This aims to enhance collective security and deter aggression from adversaries.

Agenda 47

- **Rebuilding the Military**: Agenda 47 prioritizes the rebuilding and expansion of the U.S. military to ensure it remains the most powerful force in the world. This includes increasing the defense budget and expanding the size of the armed forces.

- **Enhancing Military Technology**: Focuses on rapid development and deployment of cutting-edge military technology. This includes advancements in missile defense systems, artificial intelligence (AI), and unmanned systems.

- **Strengthening National Defense**: Emphasizes the importance of a strong national defense to protect American interests at home and abroad. This includes bolstering border security and enhancing the capabilities of the National Guard and Reserve forces.

2. Implementation Strategies

Modernization Programs:

- **Project 2025**: Advocates for comprehensive modernization programs across all branches of the military. This includes upgrading aircraft, naval vessels, ground vehicles, and communication systems. Emphasizes the integration of AI and autonomous systems to enhance operational efficiency.

- **Agenda 47**: Focuses on specific high-priority areas such as missile defense, space capabilities, and cyber warfare. This includes the development of hypersonic weapons, advanced fighter jets, and enhanced satellite systems.

Investment in Research and Development (R&D):

- **Project 2025**: Promotes increased funding for defense R&D to stay ahead of technological advancements by potential adversaries. Encourages collaboration with private sector innovators and academic institutions to accelerate innovation.

- **Agenda 47**: Prioritizes immediate investment in proven technologies while also funding experimental projects with high potential. Emphasizes the importance of maintaining technological superiority over global competitors.

Personnel and Training:

- **Project 2025**: Focuses on recruiting and retaining top talent in the military. This includes improving training programs to prepare personnel for modern warfare scenarios, such as cyber operations and electronic warfare.

- **Agenda 47**: Highlights the importance of increasing the size of the armed forces. This involves enhancing recruitment efforts and offering competitive benefits to attract and retain skilled personnel.

3. Impact on International Relations

Deterrence and Defense Posture:

- **Project 2025**: Advocates for a robust deterrence strategy to prevent aggression from adversaries. This includes maintaining a credible nuclear deterrent and forward-deploying forces in strategic locations around the world.

- **Agenda 47**: Emphasizes a strong defense posture to project power and influence globally. This includes maintaining a significant military presence in key regions such as the Asia-Pacific, Europe, and the Middle East.

Strengthening Alliances:

- **Project 2025**: Enhances military cooperation with allies through joint exercises, intelligence sharing, and defense technology transfers. This aims to build a cohesive and capable coalition to address common security challenges.

- **Agenda 47**: Focuses on renegotiating defense agreements to ensure burden-sharing among allies. This includes encouraging NATO members to meet their defense spending commitments and enhancing military cooperation with non-NATO partners.

Responding to Global Threats:

- **Project 2025**: Develops comprehensive strategies to address global threats such as terrorism, cyber attacks, and regional conflicts. This includes enhancing special operations capabilities and improving counterterrorism efforts.

- **Agenda 47**: Emphasizes a proactive approach to global threats, including preemptive measures to neutralize potential dangers. This involves increasing intelligence capabilities and improving rapid response forces.

4. Challenges and Considerations

Balancing Modernization with Budget Constraints:

- **Project 2025**: Recognizes the need to balance modernization efforts with fiscal responsibility. This involves prioritizing investments and seeking cost-effective solutions to maximize defense capabilities within budgetary limits.

- **Agenda 47**: Advocates for significant increases in defense spending to achieve rapid modernization and expansion. This includes reallocating resources from other areas of the federal budget to fund military initiatives.

Adapting to Emerging Threats:

- **Project 2025**: Emphasizes the importance of flexibility and adaptability in military planning. This includes developing capabilities to address unconventional threats such as cyber attacks and information warfare.

- **Agenda 47**: Focuses on immediate responses to emerging threats with an emphasis on maintaining a technological edge. This involves continuous assessment and adjustment of military strategies to address evolving challenges.

Ensuring Technological Superiority:

- **Project 2025**: Promotes continuous investment in cutting-edge technologies to maintain a competitive advantage. This includes fostering innovation within the defense sector and encouraging collaboration with tech companies.

- **Agenda 47**: Highlights the necessity of outpacing adversaries in technological advancements. This involves accelerating the development and deployment of next-generation weapons systems and defense platforms.

5. Future Directions

Project 2025:

- **Cyber and Space Dominance**: Emphasizes the importance of achieving dominance in cyber and space domains. This includes enhancing cyber defense capabilities and developing comprehensive space defense strategies.

- **Integration of Emerging Technologies**: Advocates for the integration of emerging technologies such as AI, quantum computing, and biotechnology into military operations to enhance capabilities and efficiency.

Agenda 47:

- **Expanding Military Capabilities**: Focuses on expanding military capabilities across all domains, including land, sea, air, space, and cyber. This involves increasing the size of the armed forces and enhancing readiness.

- **Strengthening Homeland Defense**: Prioritizes the strengthening of homeland defense capabilities to protect against domestic threats. This includes enhancing border security and improving disaster response capabilities.

Military strength and modernization are critical components of both Project 2025 and Agenda 47, reflecting the necessity of maintaining a powerful and technologically advanced military to safeguard national security. By investing in modernization programs, enhancing defense capabilities, and fostering strategic alliances, these initiatives aim to ensure the U.S. military remains unparalleled and capable of addressing both current and future threats. The emphasis on innovation, strategic partnerships, and robust defense postures underscores the importance of a strong military in promoting global stability and protecting American interests.

Cybersecurity and Technological Advancements

1. Strategic Vision and Objectives

Project 2025

- **Enhancing National Cybersecurity**: Project 2025 emphasizes the critical need for robust cybersecurity measures to protect the nation's critical infrastructure, government networks, and private sector entities from cyber attacks. The focus is on building resilient systems and developing rapid response capabilities.

- **Investing in Technological Innovation**: This initiative underscores the importance of continuous investment in technological advancements to maintain a competitive edge in defense and security. This includes advancements in artificial intelligence (AI), quantum computing, and biotechnology.

- **Promoting Public-Private Partnerships**: Encourages collaboration between government agencies and private sector leaders to foster innovation and develop comprehensive cybersecurity strategies.

Agenda 47

- **Securing American Cyberspace**: Agenda 47 prioritizes the security of America's digital infrastructure. This involves strengthening defenses against cyber threats from state and non-state actors, including hacking, espionage, and cyber warfare.

- **Technological Superiority**: Focuses on ensuring that the United States remains at the forefront of technological innovation. This includes significant investments in emerging technologies such as AI, 5G, and advanced robotics.

- **Strengthening Cyber Defense Capabilities**: Emphasizes the need for a proactive approach to cyber defense, including offensive cyber capabilities to deter and respond to cyber threats.

2. Implementation Strategies

Building a Resilient Cyber Defense Infrastructure:

- **Project 2025**: Proposes the development of a multi-layered cyber defense infrastructure that includes advanced firewalls, intrusion detection systems, and continuous monitoring. Emphasizes the importance of cybersecurity education and training for government and private sector employees.

- **Agenda 47**: Advocates for the establishment of a centralized cyber command structure to coordinate national cyber defense efforts. This includes creating rapid response teams capable of addressing cyber incidents in real-time.

Public-Private Collaboration:

- **Project 2025**: Encourages the formation of cybersecurity task forces that include representatives from government, industry, and academia. This collaboration aims to share intelligence, best practices, and develop joint strategies to enhance national cybersecurity.

- **Agenda 47**: Focuses on incentivizing private sector investment in cybersecurity through tax breaks and grants. Emphasizes the importance of industry-led innovation in developing cutting-edge cyber defense technologies.

Technological Innovation and R&D:

- **Project 2025**: Promotes significant investment in research and development (R&D) to advance cybersecurity technologies. This includes funding for academic research and partnerships with technology companies to develop new tools and techniques for cyber defense.

- **Agenda 47**: Prioritizes fast-tracking the deployment of new technologies in the field of cybersecurity. This includes supporting start-ups and innovative companies through government contracts and funding opportunities.

3. Impact on National Security

Protecting Critical Infrastructure:

- **Project 2025**: Focuses on safeguarding critical infrastructure such as power grids, financial systems, and communication networks from cyber attacks.

This includes developing redundant systems and contingency plans to ensure operational continuity in the event of a cyber incident.

- **Agenda 47**: Emphasizes the need to secure key sectors such as healthcare, transportation, and energy. This includes enhancing the cybersecurity standards for these industries and conducting regular security audits.

Deterrence and Offensive Capabilities:

- **Project 2025**: Advocates for the development of offensive cyber capabilities to deter adversaries. This includes the ability to launch retaliatory cyber attacks to disrupt the operations of hostile actors.

- **Agenda 47**: Focuses on building a robust cyber deterrence strategy that includes both defensive and offensive measures. This includes the creation of specialized cyber units within the military to carry out offensive cyber operations.

International Cooperation:

- **Project 2025**: Promotes international cooperation on cybersecurity issues. This includes working with allies to develop common cybersecurity standards and protocols, as well as sharing intelligence on cyber threats.

- **Agenda 47**: Emphasizes the importance of leading international efforts to combat cybercrime and cyber terrorism. This includes participating in global cybersecurity initiatives and forging alliances with other nations to enhance collective cyber defense.

4. Challenges and Considerations

Evolving Threat Landscape:

- **Project 2025**: Recognizes the rapidly evolving nature of cyber threats. Emphasizes the need for continuous adaptation and improvement of cyber defenses to address new and emerging threats.

- **Agenda 47**: Focuses on the importance of staying ahead of adversaries in the cyber domain. This includes maintaining technological superiority and being prepared for unconventional cyber threats.

Balancing Privacy and Security:

- **Project 2025**: Highlights the need to balance cybersecurity measures with the protection of individual privacy and civil liberties. Advocates for transparent and accountable cyber policies that respect constitutional rights.

- **Agenda 47**: Emphasizes the importance of security while ensuring that cybersecurity measures do not infringe on personal freedoms. This includes developing privacy-preserving technologies and policies.

Resource Allocation:

- **Project 2025**: Advocates for the efficient allocation of resources to maximize the effectiveness of cybersecurity initiatives. This includes prioritizing high-impact areas and avoiding duplication of efforts.

- **Agenda 47**: Focuses on securing adequate funding for cybersecurity efforts. This includes reallocating resources from less critical areas to ensure that cybersecurity remains a top priority.

5. Future Directions

Project 2025:

- **Integration of Advanced Technologies**: Promotes the integration of advanced technologies such as AI and machine learning into cybersecurity frameworks. This includes developing predictive analytics to anticipate and mitigate cyber threats.

- **Cybersecurity Workforce Development**: Emphasizes the importance of developing a skilled cybersecurity workforce. This includes funding for education and training programs to prepare the next generation of cybersecurity professionals.

Agenda 47:

- **Global Cybersecurity Leadership**: Focuses on establishing the United States as a global leader in cybersecurity. This includes leading international efforts to develop global cybersecurity standards and protocols.

- **Continued Technological Innovation**: Prioritizes ongoing investment in emerging technologies to maintain technological superiority. This includes supporting cutting-edge research and fostering innovation in the cybersecurity field.

Cybersecurity and technological advancements are critical components of both Project 2025 and Agenda 47, reflecting the necessity of protecting the nation's digital infrastructure and maintaining a competitive edge in technology. By investing in resilient cyber defense systems, fostering public-private collaboration, and promoting continuous technological innovation, these initiatives aim to ensure the United States remains secure and technologically advanced in the face of evolving cyber threats. The emphasis on strategic vision, implementation strategies, and future directions underscores the importance of cybersecurity and technological advancements in promoting national security and global stability.

Border Security and Immigration Policies

Border security and immigration policies are central components of both Project 2025 and Agenda 47, reflecting the priorities of the Heritage Foundation and Donald Trump, respectively. Both initiatives emphasize the importance of securing the nation's borders, enforcing immigration laws, and implementing policies that prioritize the safety, security, and economic well-being of American citizens. This deep dive explores the objectives, strategies, and expected impacts of border security and immigration policies under these two frameworks.

1. Objectives and Principles

Project 2025

- **Securing the Border**: The primary objective is to prevent illegal immigration and enhance national security by securing the southern border with advanced technology and increased physical barriers.

- **Enforcing Immigration Laws**: Project 2025 advocates for strict enforcement of existing immigration laws, including measures to prevent visa overstays and ensure that immigrants comply with legal entry requirements.

- **Promoting Legal Immigration**: While focusing on security, the initiative also supports a legal immigration system that benefits the economy and respects the rule of law.

Agenda 47

- **Building the Wall**: A cornerstone of Trump's agenda is the continuation and completion of the border wall along the U.S.-Mexico border to prevent illegal crossings.

- **Strengthening Immigration Enforcement**: Emphasizes the need for robust enforcement of immigration laws, including the deportation of illegal immigrants and the dismantling of sanctuary cities.

- **Reforming the Immigration System**: Advocates for a merit-based immigration system that prioritizes highly skilled immigrants who can contribute to the economy.

2. Implementation Strategies

Border Security Enhancements:

- **Project 2025**: Proposes the use of advanced technology such as drones, sensors, and surveillance systems to monitor and secure the border. Recommends increasing the number of Border Patrol agents and enhancing their training and resources.

- **Agenda 47**: Focuses on the physical construction of the border wall, combined with technological solutions to create a comprehensive security system. Advocates for increased funding and resources for the Border Patrol and Immigration and Customs Enforcement (ICE).

Legal and Administrative Measures:

- **Project 2025**: Suggests legislative reforms to close loopholes in the immigration system, such as ending chain migration and the visa lottery. Proposes reforms to the asylum system to prevent abuse and ensure that only legitimate claims are processed.

- **Agenda 47**: Calls for stricter enforcement of immigration laws, including mandatory E-Verify for employers to ensure that only legal residents are employed. Supports measures to end birthright citizenship for children of illegal immigrants.

Collaboration with State and Local Authorities:

- **Project 2025**: Encourages cooperation between federal, state, and local law enforcement agencies to enforce immigration laws effectively. Proposes grants and incentives for states that assist in immigration enforcement.

- **Agenda 47**: Advocates for cutting federal funding to sanctuary cities that refuse to cooperate with federal immigration authorities. Supports empowering local law enforcement to act as immigration officers under the 287(g) program.

3. Impact on National Security and Economy

National Security:

- **Project 2025**: Emphasizes that securing the border is essential for national security, preventing the entry of terrorists, criminals, and illegal drugs. Highlights the importance of vetting and background checks for all immigrants and asylum seekers.

- **Agenda 47**: Asserts that a secure border is vital for protecting American communities from crime and ensuring that the rule of law is upheld. Emphasizes the need for robust border security measures to prevent human trafficking and drug smuggling.

Economic Implications:

- **Project 2025**: Argues that effective border security and immigration enforcement will protect American jobs and wages by reducing illegal competition in the labor market. Supports a legal immigration system that meets the needs of the economy.

- **Agenda 47**: Focuses on the economic benefits of a merit-based immigration system that attracts highly skilled workers. Highlights the cost savings associated with reducing illegal immigration and the burden on public services.

4. Challenges and Criticisms

Balancing Security and Humanitarian Concerns:

- **Project 2025**: Acknowledges the need to balance border security with humanitarian concerns, ensuring that asylum seekers are treated fairly and humanely. Proposes measures to expedite the processing of legitimate asylum claims while deterring fraudulent ones.

- **Agenda 47**: Faces criticism for policies perceived as harsh or inhumane, such as family separations at the border. Emphasizes the need for strong deterrents to illegal immigration while addressing concerns about humane treatment.

Political and Legal Obstacles:

- **Project 2025**: Recognizes that achieving comprehensive immigration reform requires bipartisan support and may face legal challenges. Proposes a phased approach to implementing reforms and building consensus.

- **Agenda 47**: Highlights the political resistance from opponents of strict immigration policies and the legal battles over executive actions. Emphasizes the importance of appointing judges who support the administration's immigration agenda.

5. Future Directions

Comprehensive Immigration Reform:

- **Project 2025**: Advocates for comprehensive immigration reform that includes securing the border, enforcing laws, and creating a merit-based system. Emphasizes the need for a balanced approach that addresses security, economic, and humanitarian concerns.

- **Agenda 47**: Focuses on achieving long-term solutions to immigration issues through legislative and executive actions. Highlights the importance of continuing to build and enhance border security measures and reforming the immigration system.

Technological Innovations:

- **Project 2025**: Promotes the integration of new technologies in border security and immigration enforcement, such as biometric screening, AI-powered surveillance, and data analytics to improve efficiency and effectiveness.

- **Agenda 47**: Emphasizes the importance of staying ahead of evolving threats with cutting-edge technology. Advocates for continuous innovation and investment in border security infrastructure.

Conclusion

Border security and immigration policies are crucial elements of both Project 2025 and Agenda 47, reflecting the shared goals of enhancing national security, enforcing immigration laws, and promoting a legal immigration system that benefits the country. By focusing on strategic objectives, implementation strategies, and addressing challenges, these initiatives aim to create a secure and efficient immigration system that prioritizes the safety and prosperity of American citizens. The emphasis on technological innovation, collaboration with state and local authorities, and comprehensive reform highlights the commitment to achieving these goals in a balanced and effective manner.

Chapter 8   Domestic Policies
Healthcare Reforms

Healthcare reform is a critical issue for both Project 2025 of the Heritage Foundation and Agenda 47 of Donald Trump. Both initiatives prioritize restructuring the American healthcare system to make it more efficient, affordable, and patient-centered. This detailed exploration delves into the objectives, strategies, and potential impacts of healthcare reforms under these two frameworks, highlighting the emphasis on market-driven solutions, deregulation, and increasing patient choice.

1. Objectives and Principles

Project 2025

- **Market-Driven Solutions**: Advocates for a healthcare system driven by market principles where competition and consumer choice drive quality and cost-effectiveness.

- **Deregulation**: Emphasizes reducing government intervention and regulation in the healthcare sector to foster innovation and efficiency.

- **Patient-Centered Care**: Aims to put patients in control of their healthcare decisions, promoting transparency, and empowering individuals with more choices and better information.

Agenda 47

- **Repeal and Replace the Affordable Care Act (ACA)**: Aims to dismantle the ACA and replace it with a system that reduces costs and increases flexibility.

- **Reduce Prescription Drug Prices**: Focuses on lowering the cost of prescription drugs through negotiation and increased competition.

- **Increase Healthcare Access and Quality**: Emphasizes the need to expand access to healthcare while maintaining high standards of care through innovative approaches.

2. Implementation Strategies

Market-Driven Solutions:

- **Project 2025**: Proposes expanding Health Savings Accounts (HSAs) and implementing tax credits to make health insurance more affordable. Encourages the creation of Association Health Plans (AHPs) that allow small businesses to band together to purchase insurance.

- **Agenda 47**: Supports the use of block grants for Medicaid to give states more flexibility in managing healthcare funds. Promotes the expansion of telemedicine to increase access to care, especially in rural areas.

Deregulation and Reducing Costs:

- **Project 2025**: Calls for the repeal of the ACA's individual mandate and other costly regulations. Advocates for reducing the regulatory burden on healthcare providers to lower administrative costs and improve efficiency.

- **Agenda 47**: Emphasizes the need to reduce drug prices by increasing competition and allowing the importation of cheaper drugs from abroad. Supports deregulating the insurance market to increase competition and lower premiums.

Patient-Centered Reforms:

- **Project 2025**: Promotes transparency in healthcare pricing and quality to help patients make informed decisions. Supports personalized healthcare plans that cater to individual needs rather than one-size-fits-all solutions.

- **Agenda 47**: Focuses on empowering patients with more choices through the expansion of HSAs and the promotion of price transparency. Encourages innovation in healthcare delivery to improve patient outcomes and satisfaction.

3. Impact on Healthcare Access and Quality

Access to Care:

- **Project 2025**: Argues that market-driven reforms will increase access to affordable health insurance by reducing costs and expanding choices. Highlights the role of telemedicine and other innovations in improving access to care.

- **Agenda 47**: Emphasizes the importance of expanding access through deregulation and the use of block grants for Medicaid. Supports initiatives to increase the availability of affordable prescription drugs.

Quality of Care:

- **Project 2025**: Believes that competition and patient choice will drive improvements in healthcare quality. Encourages the use of evidence-based practices and innovative healthcare models to enhance care delivery.

- **Agenda 47**: Focuses on maintaining high standards of care while increasing access and reducing costs. Supports the use of technology and innovation to improve healthcare outcomes and patient experiences.

4. Challenges and Criticisms

Balancing Cost and Access:

- **Project 2025**: Faces challenges in balancing the need to reduce costs with the goal of expanding access to care. Critics argue that market-driven solutions may not adequately address the needs of low-income individuals and those with pre-existing conditions.

- **Agenda 47**: Encounters criticism for proposals to repeal the ACA, with concerns about the potential loss of coverage for millions of Americans. Emphasizes the need for a careful transition to ensure continued access to care.

Political and Legal Hurdles:

- **Project 2025**: Recognizes that significant healthcare reforms require bipartisan support and may face legal challenges. Proposes a phased approach to implementing reforms and building consensus.

- **Agenda 47**: Faces political resistance from opponents of dismantling the ACA and other healthcare regulations. Highlights the importance of appointing judges who support the administration's healthcare agenda.

5. Future Directions

Comprehensive Healthcare Reform:

- **Project 2025**: Advocates for comprehensive reform that includes market-driven solutions, deregulation, and patient-centered care. Emphasizes the need for a balanced approach that addresses cost, access, and quality.

- **Agenda 47**: Focuses on achieving long-term solutions to healthcare challenges through legislative and executive actions. Highlights the importance of continuous innovation and investment in healthcare delivery.

Technological Advancements:

- **Project 2025**: Promotes the integration of new technologies in healthcare, such as telemedicine, electronic health records, and personalized medicine.

Supports the use of data analytics to improve healthcare outcomes and efficiency.

- **Agenda 47**: Emphasizes the role of technology in increasing access to care and improving patient outcomes. Advocates for continuous investment in healthcare technology and innovation.

Healthcare reform is a pivotal aspect of both Project 2025 and Agenda 47, reflecting their shared goals of improving access, reducing costs, and enhancing the quality of care. By focusing on market-driven solutions, deregulation, and patient-centered reforms, these initiatives aim to create a more efficient and effective healthcare system. The emphasis on technological advancements, collaboration with state and local authorities, and comprehensive reform highlights the commitment to achieving these goals in a balanced and sustainable manner. Through strategic implementation and addressing challenges, Project 2025 and Agenda 47 seek to transform the American healthcare landscape for the betterment of all citizens.

Education and Workforce Development

Education and workforce development are critical components of both Project 2025 of the Heritage Foundation and Agenda 47 of Donald Trump. These initiatives aim to revitalize the American education system and strengthen the workforce to ensure long-term economic growth and global competitiveness. This comprehensive analysis delves into the objectives, strategies, and potential impacts of education and workforce development policies under these frameworks, emphasizing market-driven solutions, deregulation, and innovation.

1. Objectives and Principles

Project 2025

- **School Choice and Competition**: Advocates for policies that increase school choice and competition, such as charter schools, vouchers, and education savings accounts (ESAs).

- **Local Control and Parental Involvement**: Emphasizes the importance of local control over education decisions and greater parental involvement in their children's education.

- **Accountability and Transparency**: Calls for increased accountability and transparency in education to ensure that schools are meeting the needs of students and taxpayers.

Agenda 47

- **Reforming the Education System**: Focuses on reforming the education system to improve student outcomes and prepare them for the workforce.

- **Vocational and Technical Training**: Stresses the need for expanding vocational and technical training programs to align education with the needs of the modern economy.

- **Reducing Federal Oversight**: Aims to reduce federal oversight and return control to local communities and states.

2. Implementation Strategies

School Choice and Competition:

- **Project 2025**: Proposes expanding charter schools, vouchers, and ESAs to give parents more options for their children's education. Encourages policies that foster competition among schools to drive improvement.

- **Agenda 47**: Supports the creation and expansion of school choice programs, including tax credits for private school tuition and increased funding for charter schools. Advocates for removing barriers to school choice at the state and federal levels.

Local Control and Parental Involvement:

- **Project 2025**: Calls for devolving power from the federal government to state and local authorities, allowing them to tailor education policies to the needs of their communities. Promotes initiatives that encourage parental involvement in school decision-making processes.

- **Agenda 47**: Emphasizes the importance of local control over education and reducing the federal footprint. Supports policies that empower parents to have a greater say in their children's education through choice and accountability measures.

Accountability and Transparency:

- **Project 2025**: Advocates for robust accountability systems that measure student performance and school effectiveness. Calls for transparency in school funding and outcomes to ensure taxpayers' money is used efficiently.

- **Agenda 47**: Focuses on increasing transparency in education by requiring schools to report on student outcomes and financial expenditures. Supports accountability measures that ensure schools are meeting performance standards.

3. Impact on Education and Workforce Development

Improving Student Outcomes:

- **Project 2025**: Believes that school choice and competition will lead to better student outcomes by fostering innovation and responsiveness to student needs. Emphasizes the importance of rigorous standards and assessments to ensure quality education.

- **Agenda 47**: Aims to improve student outcomes by providing more educational options and aligning curriculum with workforce demands. Supports initiatives that focus on STEM education and other critical areas for economic growth.

Aligning Education with Workforce Needs:

- **Project 2025**: Promotes vocational and technical education programs that prepare students for high-demand jobs. Encourages partnerships between schools and industry to create pathways to employment.

- **Agenda 47**: Stresses the need for education to be aligned with the needs of the economy, including expanding apprenticeship programs and vocational training. Supports policies that incentivize schools to focus on career readiness.

4. Challenges and Criticisms

Equity and Access:

- **Project 2025**: Faces challenges in ensuring that school choice and competition do not exacerbate inequalities in education. Critics argue that these policies may lead to resource disparities between schools.

- **Agenda 47**: Encounters criticism for potentially reducing funding for public schools and widening the gap between affluent and low-income students.

Emphasizes the need for careful implementation to ensure all students benefit from reforms.

Balancing Innovation and Standards:

- **Project 2025**: Must balance the need for innovation in education with maintaining high standards and accountability. Supports the use of evidence-based practices to ensure reforms lead to improved outcomes.

- **Agenda 47**: Focuses on fostering innovation while maintaining rigorous standards. Encourages the use of data and research to inform education policies and practices.

Political and Legal Hurdles:

- **Project 2025**: Recognizes that significant education reforms require bipartisan support and may face legal challenges. Proposes a collaborative approach to building consensus for policy changes.

- **Agenda 47**: Faces political resistance from opponents of reducing federal oversight and expanding school choice. Highlights the importance of appointing education leaders who support the administration's vision.

5. Future Directions

Expanding Access to Quality Education:

- **Project 2025**: Advocates for expanding access to high-quality education through school choice, charter schools, and other innovative models.

Emphasizes the importance of continuous improvement and adaptability in education.

- **Agenda 47**: Focuses on ensuring all students have access to quality education, regardless of their socioeconomic status. Supports policies that incentivize schools to improve and innovate.

Strengthening Workforce Development:

- **Project 2025**: Promotes lifelong learning and skills development to prepare the workforce for the demands of the modern economy. Encourages collaboration between education institutions and employers to create pathways to employment.

- **Agenda 47**: Emphasizes the need for a robust workforce development system that includes vocational training, apprenticeships, and on-the-job training. Supports policies that align education with the needs of the economy and promote economic growth.

Education and workforce development are foundational elements of both Project 2025 and Agenda 47, reflecting their shared commitment to improving the American education system and preparing the workforce for the future. By focusing on school choice, local control, accountability, and alignment with economic needs, these initiatives aim to create a more effective and responsive education system. The emphasis on innovation, transparency, and community involvement highlights the potential for transformative change in education and workforce development. Through strategic implementation and addressing challenges, Project 2025 and Agenda 47 seek to ensure that all Americans have the opportunity to succeed in a dynamic and competitive global economy.

Social and Cultural Policies

Social and cultural policies are integral components of both Project 2025 of the Heritage Foundation and Agenda 47 of Donald Trump. These initiatives aim to shape the cultural landscape of America by emphasizing traditional values, promoting national identity, and addressing contentious social issues. This detailed analysis explores the objectives, strategies, and potential impacts of social and cultural policies under these frameworks, highlighting their significance in fostering a cohesive and resilient society.

1. Objectives and Principles

Project 2025 (Heritage Foundation):

- **Promoting Traditional Values**: Emphasizes the importance of traditional family structures, religious freedom, and moral values in shaping society.

- **Preserving National Identity**: Advocates for policies that strengthen national identity and patriotism.

- **Addressing Social Issues**: Focuses on solutions to pressing social issues such as crime, drug addiction, and homelessness through conservative approaches.

Agenda 47

- **Defending American Values**: Stresses the need to defend and promote American values, including freedom of speech, religious liberty, and the right to bear arms.

- **Strengthening Community and National Unity**: Promotes policies that foster community cohesion and national unity.

- **Tackling Social Challenges**: Aims to address social challenges by implementing policies that support law enforcement, reduce crime, and combat substance abuse.

2. Implementation Strategies

Promoting Traditional Values:

- **Project 2025**: Encourages policies that support traditional family structures, such as marriage between a man and a woman and parental rights in education. Advocates for religious freedom protections and faith-based initiatives.

- **Agenda 47**: Supports measures that uphold traditional values, including protecting religious liberties and opposing policies perceived as undermining family structures. Emphasizes the importance of Judeo-Christian values in public life.

Preserving National Identity:

- **Project 2025**: Proposes initiatives that promote patriotism and civic education, including curriculum reforms that emphasize American history and civics. Supports measures that protect national symbols and heritage sites.

- **Agenda 47**: Advocates for policies that reinforce national identity, such as promoting patriotic education and opposing efforts to revise historical narratives. Supports the preservation of national monuments and cultural heritage.

Addressing Social Issues:

- **Project 2025**: Calls for conservative approaches to address social issues, including tougher law enforcement, stricter sentencing for criminals, and initiatives to reduce drug addiction and homelessness. Supports community-based solutions and private sector involvement.

- **Agenda 47**: Focuses on policies that enhance public safety, such as increasing support for law enforcement, implementing criminal justice reforms, and combating drug trafficking. Promotes rehabilitation programs and community outreach to address addiction and homelessness.

3. Impact on Society and Culture

Strengthening Family and Community:

- **Project 2025**: Believes that promoting traditional family structures and values will lead to stronger, more cohesive communities. Emphasizes the role of families in providing stability and support.

- **Agenda 47**: Aims to strengthen families and communities by upholding traditional values and providing support for parental rights and religious freedoms. Advocates for policies that foster community engagement and civic responsibility.

Enhancing National Unity and Patriotism:

- **Project 2025**: Promotes initiatives that foster national unity and pride, such as patriotic education and the preservation of cultural heritage. Believes that a strong national identity is essential for social cohesion.

- **Agenda 47**: Emphasizes the importance of national unity and patriotism in maintaining social order and resilience. Supports measures that celebrate American values and history.

Reducing Crime and Social Issues:

- **Project 2025**: Advocates for conservative approaches to reducing crime and social issues, such as tougher sentencing, increased support for law enforcement, and community-based solutions to addiction and homelessness.

- **Agenda 47**: Focuses on policies that enhance public safety and address social challenges through law enforcement support, criminal justice reforms, and rehabilitation programs. Believes that a strong stance on crime and social issues will lead to safer communities.

4. Challenges and Criticisms

Balancing Tradition and Progress:

- **Project 2025**: Faces criticism for potentially prioritizing traditional values over progressive social reforms. Critics argue that this approach may not address the needs of a diverse and evolving society.

- **Agenda 47**: Encounters challenges in balancing the promotion of traditional values with the demands of a modern, diverse population. Emphasizes the need for policies that respect individual freedoms while upholding societal norms.

Addressing Social Inequality:

- **Project 2025**: Critics argue that conservative approaches to social issues may not adequately address underlying social inequalities. Emphasizes the importance of community-based solutions and private sector involvement.

- **Agenda 47**: Faces criticism for potentially overlooking systemic issues that contribute to social inequality. Supports policies that provide opportunities for all individuals to succeed while maintaining law and order.

Political and Legal Obstacles:

- **Project 2025**: Recognizes that implementing conservative social policies may face political resistance and legal challenges. Proposes a collaborative approach to building consensus and enacting reforms.

- **Agenda 47**: Encounters political opposition from those who disagree with its emphasis on traditional values and law enforcement. Highlights the importance of appointing leaders who share the administration's vision.

5. Future Directions

Promoting Civic Education and Engagement:

- **Project 2025**: Advocates for expanding civic education programs that emphasize American history, government, and civic responsibility. Supports initiatives that encourage community involvement and volunteerism.

- **Agenda 47**: Focuses on enhancing civic education to foster a sense of national pride and responsibility. Supports policies that promote engagement in community and public service.

Addressing Emerging Social Issues:

- **Project 2025**: Emphasizes the need to adapt conservative social policies to address emerging issues, such as the impact of technology on society and changing family dynamics. Supports ongoing research and innovation in social policy.

- **Agenda 47**: Aims to address new social challenges by updating policies to reflect current realities. Supports initiatives that leverage technology and innovation to improve social outcomes.

Strengthening National Identity and Unity:

- **Project 2025**: Promotes ongoing efforts to strengthen national identity and unity through education, cultural preservation, and community engagement. Believes that a cohesive national identity is essential for social stability.

- **Agenda 47**: Emphasizes the importance of national unity in maintaining a strong and resilient society. Supports policies that celebrate American values and history while promoting inclusivity and diversity.

Social and cultural policies are central to the visions of both Project 2025 and Agenda 47, reflecting their commitment to promoting traditional values, preserving national identity, and addressing social issues. By focusing on family structures, community cohesion, and national unity, these initiatives aim to create a more resilient and cohesive society. The emphasis on conservative approaches to social challenges highlights the potential for transformative change in addressing crime, addiction, and homelessness. Through strategic implementation and addressing challenges, Project 2025 and Agenda 47 seek to ensure that America's social and cultural landscape remains vibrant, inclusive, and reflective of its core values.

Chapter 9   Energy and Environment
Energy Independence and Innovation

E nergy independence and innovation are pivotal aspects of both Project 2025 of the Heritage Foundation and Agenda 47 of Donald Trump. These initiatives aim to reduce America's dependence on foreign energy sources, enhance energy security, and foster technological advancements in the energy sector. This comprehensive analysis explores the objectives, strategies, and potential impacts of energy policies under these frameworks, highlighting their significance in securing America's energy future.

1. Objectives and Principles

Project 2025

- **Achieving Energy Independence**: Aims to make the U.S. self-sufficient in energy production by increasing domestic oil, natural gas, and coal production.

- **Promoting Free Market Principles**: Advocates for reducing government intervention in the energy market to encourage competition and innovation.

- **Enhancing Energy Security**: Focuses on securing critical energy infrastructure and diversifying energy sources to protect against disruptions.

Agenda 47

- **Maximizing Domestic Energy Production**: Emphasizes expanding exploration and production of oil, natural gas, and coal to achieve energy independence.

- **Deregulating the Energy Sector**: Supports rolling back regulations that are seen as hindering energy production and investment.

- **Investing in Energy Innovation**: Encourages investment in new energy technologies, including renewable energy sources and advanced fossil fuel technologies.

2. Implementation Strategies

Increasing Domestic Production:

- **Project 2025**: Advocates for expanding oil and natural gas drilling on federal lands and offshore areas. Supports policies that streamline permitting processes and reduce regulatory barriers for energy projects.

- **Agenda 47**: Promotes policies that open up new areas for oil and gas exploration, including the Arctic National Wildlife Refuge (ANWR) and offshore regions. Supports incentives for increasing coal production and reviving the coal industry.

Reducing Regulatory Burdens:

- **Project 2025**: Calls for a comprehensive review and rollback of regulations that are deemed to hinder energy production and economic growth. Emphasizes the need for regulatory certainty to attract investment.

- **Agenda 47**: Focuses on eliminating regulations imposed during previous administrations that are perceived as overly restrictive. Advocates for a regulatory framework that balances environmental protection with economic growth.

Promoting Technological Innovation:

- **Project 2025**: Encourages investment in research and development (R&D) to advance energy technologies, including carbon capture and storage (CCS), advanced nuclear power, and renewable energy. Supports public-private partnerships to drive innovation.

- **Agenda 47**: Emphasizes the need for technological advancements in the energy sector, including next-generation fossil fuel technologies and renewable energy solutions. Supports tax incentives and funding for energy R&D initiatives.

Enhancing Energy Infrastructure:

- **Project 2025**: Focuses on modernizing and expanding energy infrastructure, including pipelines, refineries, and the electric grid. Supports policies that enhance the resilience and security of energy infrastructure.

- **Agenda 47**: Advocates for significant investments in energy infrastructure projects to improve energy transportation and distribution. Supports initiatives to protect critical infrastructure from cyber threats and physical attacks.

Diversifying Energy Sources:

- **Project 2025**: Promotes a diversified energy portfolio that includes fossil fuels, nuclear power, and renewable energy. Supports policies that encourage the development of all energy sources to enhance energy security.

- **Agenda 47**: Emphasizes the importance of a balanced energy mix, including traditional and renewable energy sources. Supports policies that incentivize the development of new energy technologies and diversify the energy supply.

3. Impact on Energy Security and Economy

Enhancing Energy Security:

- **Project 2025**: Believes that increasing domestic energy production and diversifying energy sources will reduce America's vulnerability to global energy market fluctuations and geopolitical risks. Supports policies that enhance the resilience of energy infrastructure.

- **Agenda 47**: Aims to achieve energy independence by maximizing domestic energy production and reducing reliance on foreign oil. Emphasizes the importance of energy security in national security and economic stability.

Driving Economic Growth:

- **Project 2025**: Advocates for policies that boost economic growth by creating jobs in the energy sector, reducing energy costs, and attracting investment. Emphasizes the economic benefits of a robust domestic energy industry.

- **Agenda 47**: Focuses on revitalizing the energy sector as a key driver of economic growth. Supports policies that increase energy production, lower energy prices, and create high-paying jobs in the energy industry.

Fostering Innovation and Competitiveness:

- **Project 2025**: Believes that promoting technological innovation in the energy sector will enhance America's global competitiveness and leadership in energy technologies. Supports initiatives that drive innovation and improve energy efficiency.

- **Agenda 47**: Emphasizes the need for America to lead in energy innovation and technology. Supports policies that foster a competitive energy market and encourage private sector investment in new energy technologies.

4. Challenges and Criticisms

Environmental Concerns:

- **Project 2025**: Faces criticism from environmental groups for promoting fossil fuel production and reducing environmental regulations. Advocates for a balanced approach that considers environmental protection and economic growth.

- **Agenda 47**: Encounters opposition from those who argue that expanding fossil fuel production and rolling back regulations will have negative environmental impacts. Emphasizes the need to balance energy development with environmental stewardship.

Balancing Energy Development and Conservation:

- **Project 2025**: Recognizes the challenge of balancing energy development with conservation efforts. Supports policies that protect environmentally sensitive areas while promoting responsible energy production.

- **Agenda 47**: Advocates for policies that balance energy development with environmental conservation. Emphasizes the importance of responsible resource management and minimizing environmental impacts.

Political and Legal Obstacles:

- **Project 2025**: Faces potential political and legal challenges in implementing energy policies, particularly from states and local governments with different energy priorities. Supports building consensus and addressing stakeholder concerns.

- **Agenda 47**: Encounters political opposition from those who disagree with its energy policies. Highlights the importance of appointing leaders and judges who support the administration's vision for energy independence.

5. Future Directions

Advancing Renewable Energy:

- **Project 2025**: Encourages continued investment in renewable energy sources, such as wind, solar, and hydroelectric power. Supports policies that promote renewable energy development and integration into the energy grid.

- **Agenda 47**: Emphasizes the importance of renewable energy in achieving a balanced energy mix. Supports incentives for renewable energy projects and research into new renewable technologies.

Improving Energy Efficiency:

- **Project 2025**: Advocates for policies that enhance energy efficiency in buildings, transportation, and industry. Supports initiatives that reduce energy consumption and improve overall energy productivity.

- **Agenda 47**: Focuses on improving energy efficiency as a key component of energy policy. Supports programs that promote energy-saving technologies and practices across various sectors.

Strengthening International Energy Cooperation:

- **Project 2025**: Promotes international cooperation on energy issues, including trade, technology exchange, and joint research initiatives. Supports policies that enhance global energy security and stability.

- **Agenda 47**: Emphasizes the importance of international partnerships in achieving energy security. Supports bilateral and multilateral agreements that promote energy cooperation and address global energy challenges.

Energy independence and innovation are central to the visions of both Project 2025 and Agenda 47, reflecting their commitment to securing America's energy future. By focusing on increasing domestic production, reducing regulatory burdens, and promoting technological innovation, these initiatives aim to enhance energy security, drive economic growth, and foster a competitive energy market. The emphasis on balancing energy development with environmental protection highlights the potential for sustainable energy policies. Through strategic implementation and addressing challenges, Project 2025 and Agenda 47 seek to ensure that America remains a leader in energy production, innovation, and security.

Environmental Policies and Sustainability

Environmental policies and sustainability are crucial components of both Project 2025 of the Heritage Foundation and Agenda 47 of Donald Trump. These initiatives aim to balance economic growth with environmental stewardship, ensuring that natural resources are managed responsibly and sustainably. This comprehensive analysis explores the objectives, strategies, and potential impacts of environmental policies under these frameworks, highlighting their significance in promoting sustainability and protecting the environment.

1. Objectives and Principles

Project 2025

- **Promoting Environmental Stewardship**: Focuses on responsible management of natural resources and conservation efforts.

- **Balancing Economic Growth and Environmental Protection**: Seeks to harmonize economic development with environmental sustainability.

- **Reducing Regulatory Burdens**: Aims to streamline environmental regulations to foster innovation and economic activity.

Agenda 47

- **Ensuring Clean Air and Water**: Commits to maintaining high standards for air and water quality.

- **Encouraging Sustainable Resource Use**: Promotes the sustainable use of natural resources through innovation and technological advancements.

- **Rolling Back Overreaching Regulations**: Focuses on reducing regulatory constraints that are viewed as hindering economic growth.

2. Implementation Strategies

Regulatory Reforms:

- **Project 2025**: Advocates for a comprehensive review of existing environmental regulations to eliminate those that are considered overly burdensome. Emphasizes the need for regulatory certainty to encourage investment and innovation.

- **Agenda 47**: Supports rolling back regulations imposed during previous administrations that are seen as excessive. Promotes a balanced regulatory framework that protects the environment while supporting economic growth.

Promoting Technological Innovation:

- **Project 2025**: Encourages investment in research and development (R&D) to advance environmental technologies, including clean energy and pollution control. Supports public-private partnerships to drive innovation.

- **Agenda 47**: Emphasizes the role of technological advancements in achieving environmental goals. Supports tax incentives and funding for R&D in environmental technologies.

Enhancing Conservation Efforts:

- **Project 2025**: Focuses on conserving natural habitats and biodiversity through sustainable land management practices. Supports policies that incentivize private land conservation.

- **Agenda 47**: Promotes conservation initiatives that protect natural resources while allowing for responsible economic use. Encourages public-private partnerships in conservation efforts.

Encouraging Market-Based Solutions:

- **Project 2025**: Advocates for market-based approaches to environmental protection, such as emissions trading and conservation banking. Supports policies that leverage market mechanisms to achieve environmental goals.

- **Agenda 47**: Emphasizes the importance of free-market principles in addressing environmental challenges. Supports initiatives that use market incentives to promote sustainability.

Reducing Carbon Emissions:

- **Project 2025**: Promotes policies that reduce carbon emissions through technological innovation and energy efficiency. Supports voluntary programs and incentives for businesses to reduce their carbon footprint.

- **Agenda 47**: Focuses on reducing carbon emissions without imposing restrictive regulations. Encourages the development of clean energy technologies and practices.

3. Impact on Environmental Sustainability

Improving Air and Water Quality:

- **Project 2025**: Believes that technological advancements and regulatory reforms will improve air and water quality. Supports policies that enhance monitoring and enforcement of environmental standards.

- **Agenda 47**: Aims to maintain high standards for air and water quality through innovative solutions and deregulation. Emphasizes the importance of clean air and water for public health and economic growth.

Promoting Renewable Energy:

- **Project 2025**: Encourages the development and integration of renewable energy sources, such as wind, solar, and hydroelectric power. Supports policies that promote renewable energy development and reduce dependence on fossil fuels.

- **Agenda 47**: Emphasizes the role of renewable energy in achieving a balanced energy mix. Supports incentives for renewable energy projects and research into new renewable technologies.

Enhancing Energy Efficiency:

- **Project 2025**: Advocates for policies that enhance energy efficiency in buildings, transportation, and industry. Supports initiatives that reduce energy consumption and improve overall energy productivity.

- **Agenda 47**: Focuses on improving energy efficiency as a key component of environmental policy. Supports programs that promote energy-saving technologies and practices across various sectors.

Protecting Natural Habitats and Biodiversity:

- **Project 2025**: Promotes conservation efforts that protect natural habitats and biodiversity. Supports policies that incentivize private land conservation and sustainable land management practices.

- **Agenda 47**: Emphasizes the importance of protecting natural resources and biodiversity. Encourages public-private partnerships in conservation initiatives and sustainable resource management.

4. Challenges and Criticisms

Balancing Economic Growth and Environmental Protection:

- **Project 2025**: Faces criticism from environmental groups for prioritizing economic growth over environmental protection. Advocates for a balanced approach that considers both economic and environmental objectives.

- **Agenda 47**: Encounters opposition from those who argue that deregulation and increased fossil fuel production will harm the environment. Emphasizes the need to balance economic development with environmental stewardship.

Addressing Climate Change:

- **Project 2025**: Recognizes the challenge of addressing climate change while promoting economic growth. Supports voluntary measures and technological innovation to reduce carbon emissions.

- **Agenda 47**: Faces criticism for not taking more aggressive action on climate change. Emphasizes the importance of economic growth and energy security in addressing environmental challenges.

Political and Legal Obstacles:

- **Project 2025**: Faces potential political and legal challenges in implementing environmental policies, particularly from states and local governments with different environmental priorities. Supports building consensus and addressing stakeholder concerns.

- **Agenda 47**: Encounters political opposition from those who disagree with its environmental policies. Highlights the importance of appointing leaders and judges who support the administration's vision for environmental protection and economic growth.

5. Future Directions

Advancing Clean Energy Technologies:

- **Project 2025**: Encourages continued investment in clean energy technologies, including wind, solar, and advanced nuclear power. Supports policies that promote the development and integration of clean energy into the energy grid.

- **Agenda 47**: Emphasizes the importance of clean energy in achieving environmental and economic goals. Supports incentives for clean energy projects and research into new clean energy technologies.

Promoting Sustainable Agriculture:

- **Project 2025**: Advocates for sustainable agricultural practices that protect natural resources and promote food security. Supports policies that incentivize sustainable farming and reduce environmental impacts.

- **Agenda 47**: Focuses on promoting sustainable agriculture as a key component of environmental policy. Encourages initiatives that support sustainable farming practices and reduce environmental impacts.

Enhancing Environmental Education and Awareness:

- **Project 2025**: Believes in the importance of environmental education and awareness in promoting sustainability. Supports programs that educate the public about environmental issues and encourage sustainable practices.

- **Agenda 47**: Emphasizes the role of education in achieving environmental goals. Supports initiatives that raise awareness about environmental challenges and promote sustainable behaviors.

Strengthening International Environmental Cooperation:

- **Project 2025**: Promotes international cooperation on environmental issues, including climate change, biodiversity conservation, and pollution control. Supports policies that enhance global environmental sustainability.

- **Agenda 47**: Emphasizes the importance of international partnerships in addressing environmental challenges. Supports bilateral and multilateral agreements that promote environmental cooperation and sustainability.

Environmental policies and sustainability are integral to the visions of both Project 2025 and Agenda 47, reflecting their commitment to balancing economic growth with environmental stewardship. By focusing on regulatory reforms, technological innovation, and conservation efforts, these initiatives aim to promote sustainability, protect natural resources, and enhance environmental quality. The emphasis on market-based solutions and private sector engagement highlights the potential for innovative and sustainable environmental policies. Through strategic implementation and addressing challenges, Project 2025 and Agenda 47 seek to ensure that America remains a leader in environmental protection and sustainability.

Balancing Economic Growth and Environmental Protection

B alancing economic growth with environmental protection is a complex challenge addressed by Project 2025 of the Heritage Foundation and Agenda 47 of Donald Trump. These initiatives aim to foster economic prosperity while ensuring responsible stewardship of natural resources and environmental sustainability. This exploration delves into their strategies, approaches, and the broader implications of their policies on achieving this delicate balance.

1. Project 2025

Objectives and Strategies:

- **Promoting Regulatory Certainty**: Advocates for clear and predictable environmental regulations to provide stability for businesses while safeguarding environmental quality.

- **Encouraging Innovation**: Supports technological advancements and innovation in environmental technologies to mitigate environmental impact without stifling economic growth.

- **Incentivizing Conservation**: Promotes voluntary conservation efforts and incentives for sustainable land use practices to preserve natural habitats and biodiversity.

- **Market-Based Solutions**: Emphasizes market-driven approaches such as emissions trading and conservation banking to achieve environmental goals efficiently.

- **Energy Independence**: Promotes energy independence through diverse energy sources, including renewable energy, while enhancing energy efficiency standards.

Challenges and Criticisms:

- **Criticism from Environmental Groups**: Faces criticism for potentially prioritizing economic growth over stringent environmental regulations, raising concerns about long-term environmental impacts.

- **Legal and Political Challenges**: Encounters legal and political obstacles in implementing regulatory reforms and balancing state and federal environmental priorities.

2. Agenda 47

Objectives and Strategies:

- **Rolling Back Regulations**: Focuses on deregulation to reduce perceived regulatory burdens on industries, aiming to spur economic growth while ensuring compliance with minimal environmental standards.

- **Energy Dominance**: Advocates for increased domestic energy production, including fossil fuels, to achieve energy independence and reduce reliance on foreign sources.

- **Environmental Policy Alignment**: Seeks to align environmental policies with economic objectives, emphasizing job creation and infrastructure development.

- **Strengthening Enforcement**: Enhances enforcement of existing environmental regulations to ensure compliance and protect air and water quality.

- **Promoting Technological Advancements**: Supports technological advancements in clean energy and pollution control technologies to address environmental challenges while promoting economic growth.

Challenges and Criticisms:

- **Environmental Impact Concerns**: Faces criticism for potentially weakening environmental protections in favor of economic gains, raising concerns about air and water quality, and biodiversity conservation.

- **International Relations**: Engages in negotiations and agreements to address environmental issues that may impact global trade, international relations, and economic stability.

3. Strategies for Balancing Economic Growth and Environmental Protection

Integration of Sustainable Practices:

- **Project 2025**: Integrates sustainable practices into business operations through incentives for energy efficiency, waste reduction, and conservation efforts.

- **Agenda 47**: Promotes sustainable practices through technological advancements and market-based solutions that minimize environmental impact while maximizing economic benefits.

Investment in Clean Technologies:

- **Project 2025**: Invests in research and development of clean technologies such as renewable energy, carbon capture, and energy-efficient technologies to reduce environmental footprint.

- **Agenda 47**: Supports private-sector investment in clean technologies and innovative solutions to address environmental challenges without imposing stringent regulations.

Public-Private Partnerships:

- **Project 2025**: Encourages collaboration between government agencies, private sectors, and non-profit organizations to implement sustainable initiatives and achieve environmental objectives.

- **Agenda 47**: Promotes partnerships to leverage resources, expertise, and technology to enhance environmental protection and economic growth.

Enhanced Regulatory Framework:

- **Project 2025**: Develops a balanced regulatory framework that considers environmental impact, economic feasibility, and technological advancements to achieve sustainable development goals.

- **Agenda 47**: Simplifies regulatory processes and enhances regulatory certainty to stimulate economic growth while maintaining environmental safeguards.

4. Impact on Economic Development and Environmental Sustainability

Economic Growth:

- **Project 2025**: Supports economic growth through sustainable practices that attract investment, create jobs, and enhance economic resilience.

- **Agenda 47**: Focuses on job creation and economic development through energy dominance and infrastructure projects while addressing environmental concerns.

Environmental Sustainability:

- **Project 2025**: Promotes long-term environmental sustainability through conservation efforts, renewable energy adoption, and pollution reduction initiatives.

- **Agenda 47**: Seeks to balance economic development with environmental protection through strategic policy alignment and technological innovation.

Achieving a balance between economic growth and environmental protection requires strategic planning, innovative approaches, and stakeholder engagement. Project 2025 and Agenda 47 exemplify different approaches to addressing this challenge, each aiming to promote economic prosperity while safeguarding natural resources and environmental quality. By leveraging technology, market-based solutions, and sustainable practices, these initiatives strive to create a future where economic development coexists harmoniously with environmental sustainability.

Chapter 10   Judicial and Legal Reforms
Supreme Court and Judicial Appointments

Project 2025, a strategic initiative of the Heritage Foundation during the Trump administration, emphasized the importance of appointing judges who adhere strictly to originalist and textualist interpretations of the Constitution. This perspective viewed the judiciary as a branch of government tasked with interpreting laws rather than creating them. According to Project 2025, the appointment of justices committed to these principles was essential to curb perceived judicial activism and restore a more restrained judicial approach. This viewpoint sought to prioritize fidelity to the Constitution's original intent and textual meaning, ensuring that judicial decisions aligned closely with the framers' intentions and legal precedent.

Agenda 47's Position on Judicial Appointments:

Under Agenda 47, a broader framework encompassing Project 2025, the approach to judicial appointments was framed within the context of restoring constitutional norms and limiting the scope of judicial discretion. Agenda 47 proponents advocated for nominees who demonstrated a commitment to upholding conservative legal principles, including originalism and textualism. This perspective aimed to counterbalance what they perceived as a trend toward judicial activism that had, in their view, expanded the judiciary's role beyond its constitutional bounds. By promoting judges with a strict interpretation of the law, Agenda 47 sought to safeguard individual liberties, uphold the separation of powers, and promote a judiciary that respects legislative authority and societal norms.

Public and Critical Reception

The initiatives of Project 2025 and Agenda 47 generated significant debate and scrutiny among legal scholars, policymakers, and the public. Supporters applauded these efforts as necessary steps to restore constitutional fidelity and judicial restraint, arguing that such appointments would ensure a judiciary more closely aligned with the framers' vision. Critics, however, voiced concerns that prioritizing originalism and textualism could lead to setbacks in civil rights, environmental protections, and other progressive legal advancements. They argued that a more flexible approach to interpreting the Constitution was essential to address evolving societal needs and challenges.

National Importance and Future Implications:

The impact of Project 2025 and Agenda 47 on Supreme Court and judicial appointments extends beyond partisan politics, influencing the trajectory of American jurisprudence for years to come. These initiatives underscore the enduring significance of judicial philosophy in shaping legal precedent, national policy, and the protection of individual rights. As the judiciary continues to evolve, the legacy of these appointments will continue to shape the contours of constitutional interpretation and judicial decision-making, reflecting broader debates about the role of the courts in American democracy.

Project 2025 and Agenda 47 articulated distinct perspectives on Supreme Court and judicial appointments, advocating for a judiciary grounded in originalist and textualist principles. Understanding these viewpoints is essential for comprehending the ideological underpinnings and lasting implications of these initiatives on the American legal landscape.

Legal Reforms and Civil Liberties

L egal reforms pertaining to civil liberties are critical aspects of governance, influencing societal norms, individual rights, and the balance between state authority and personal freedoms. Project 2025 and Agenda 47, spearheaded by the Heritage Foundation under the Trump administration, aimed to influence these areas significantly.

Project 2025's Approach to Legal Reforms:

Project 2025 advocated for legal reforms that aligned with conservative principles, particularly emphasizing originalism and textualism in judicial interpretation. This approach asserts that the Constitution should be interpreted based on its original meaning at the time it was drafted and ratified. Supporters of Project 2025 argued that adherence to these principles promotes judicial restraint, limits the potential for judicial activism, and ensures that laws are interpreted according to their original intent rather than evolving societal norms. From this perspective, legal reforms are seen as essential to preserving constitutional rights and maintaining a judiciary that upholds the rule of law without overstepping its bounds.

Agenda 47's Impact on Civil Liberties:

Agenda 47, within which Project 2025 operated, sought to address perceived overreach by the judiciary and federal agencies that could infringe upon civil liberties. This agenda promoted reforms aimed at reducing government regulation, protecting religious freedoms, and safeguarding Second Amendment rights, among other conservative priorities. Advocates argued that these reforms were necessary to preserve individual liberties from encroachment by an increasingly expansive government.

Criticism and Opposition

Critics of Project 2025 and Agenda 47 voiced concerns about potential setbacks to civil liberties and progressive legal advancements. They argued that strict adherence to originalism and textualism could limit the judiciary's ability to adapt to changing societal values and emerging issues, potentially undermining protections for marginalized communities and hindering progress on issues such as LGBTQ+ rights, reproductive rights, and environmental protections.

Public Perception and Debate

The initiatives under Project 2025 and Agenda 47 sparked heated public debate and scrutiny. Supporters viewed these efforts as essential for restoring constitutional norms, protecting individual freedoms, and curbing what they saw as government overreach. Opponents cautioned against rolling back hard-won legal protections and warned of the potential consequences for civil rights and equality under the law.

National Significance and Long-term Impact

Legal reforms and debates over civil liberties have profound implications for the nation's legal framework, governance, and social cohesion. The outcomes of these reforms shape legal precedents, influence public policy, and define the boundaries of governmental authority and individual rights. As such, understanding the nuances of these debates is crucial for comprehending the evolving landscape of civil liberties and the ongoing struggle to balance individual freedoms with societal responsibilities.

legal reforms and civil liberties are central to the ideological agendas of Project 2025 and Agenda 47, reflecting broader debates about constitutional interpretation, judicial philosophy, and the role of government in protecting individual rights.

These initiatives continue to shape the legal landscape in the United States and provoke discussions about the balance between liberty and governance in a democratic society.

Criminal Justice and Law Enforcement

Criminal justice and law enforcement policies are crucial components of governance, influencing public safety, individual rights, and societal trust in the justice system. Project 2025 and Agenda 47, initiatives under the Heritage Foundation during the Trump administration, aimed to shape these areas significantly.

Project 2025's Approach to Criminal Justice:

Project 2025 advocated for reforms that emphasized law and order, with a focus on enhancing public safety through tougher sentencing policies and a robust law enforcement approach. This perspective viewed crime reduction as a priority, supporting measures such as mandatory minimum sentences, increased funding for police departments, and initiatives to combat illegal immigration and drug trafficking. Supporters argued that these policies were necessary to deter crime, protect communities, and uphold the rule of law.

Agenda 47's Impact on Law Enforcement:

Within Agenda 47, efforts were directed at bolstering law enforcement capabilities and supporting officers in their duties. This included advocating for policies that prioritize the safety and well-being of law enforcement personnel, such as providing resources for training, equipment, and support services. Agenda 47 also focused on enhancing collaboration between federal, state, and local law enforcement agencies to address complex criminal threats effectively.

Criticism and Opposition:

Critics of Project 2025 and Agenda 47 raised concerns about potential issues such as racial disparities in policing and sentencing, the impact of tough-on-crime policies on marginalized communities, and the need for comprehensive reforms to address root causes of crime. They argued that overly punitive measures could exacerbate societal inequalities and strain relationships between law enforcement and the communities they serve.

Public Perception and Debate:

The initiatives under Project 2025 and Agenda 47 sparked significant public debate and controversy. Supporters applauded efforts to strengthen law enforcement and prioritize public safety, viewing these measures as essential for maintaining order and protecting citizens' rights. Opponents called for more nuanced approaches that balance crime prevention with addressing systemic issues within the criminal justice system, such as reforming bail practices, reducing incarceration rates, and promoting rehabilitation programs.

National Significance and Long-term Impact:

Criminal justice and law enforcement policies have far-reaching implications for national security, community well-being, and the administration of justice. The outcomes of these policies shape public trust in law enforcement, influence crime rates, and define the standards of fairness and accountability within the legal system. Understanding the complexities of these issues is crucial for policymakers, law enforcement officials, and the public as they navigate the challenges and opportunities in shaping a just and equitable society.

In conclusion, criminal justice and law enforcement policies under Project 2025 and Agenda 47 reflect divergent approaches to addressing crime and maintaining public safety. These initiatives continue to shape national discourse on issues of policing, sentencing, and community relations with law enforcement. As the country navigates evolving societal needs and challenges, ongoing dialogue and thoughtful policy considerations are essential for achieving a balanced and effective criminal justice system that serves all Americans fairly.

Chapter 11   Public Opinion and Media
Influence of Media on Public Perception

The media plays a pivotal role in shaping public opinion and perception, influencing how individuals perceive events, policies, and public figures. This discussion delves into the multifaceted ways through which media channels, both traditional and digital, impact public perception.

1. Media Channels and Reach

Traditional Media:

- Newspapers, television, and radio historically dominated public discourse, disseminating news and editorial content that framed public understanding.

- Editorial Control: Editors and journalists curated content, influencing public sentiment through selective coverage and framing.

Digital Media:

- Rise of Social Media: Platforms like Facebook, Twitter, and YouTube democratized information dissemination, allowing for rapid sharing and viral content.

- Influence of Algorithms: Algorithms personalize content, creating filter bubbles that reinforce existing beliefs and perceptions.

2. Agenda Setting and Framing

Agenda Setting:

- Media Agenda: Determines which topics receive extensive coverage, influencing public awareness and prioritization of issues.

- Political Agenda: Media coverage of political campaigns and policies shapes public discourse and voter priorities.

Framing:

- Media Frames: Presenting issues through specific lenses (e.g., economic, social justice) influences how audiences interpret and respond to news.

- Framing Effects: Impact on public perception of policy effectiveness, morality, and societal norms.

3. Influence on Political Perception

Political Campaigns:

- Media Coverage: Shapes voter perception of candidates, policies, and campaign strategies.

- Media Bias: Perceived bias in reporting can sway public trust and influence electoral outcomes.

4. Impact on Social Issues

Social Movements:

- Media Amplification: Coverage of social movements (e.g., #MeToo, Black Lives Matter) amplifies public awareness and mobilizes support.

- Public Discourse: Media portrayal influences societal attitudes towards diversity, equality, and social justice issues.

5. Trust in Media and Misinformation

Media Credibility:

- Trust Issues: Public perception of media credibility affects receptivity to news and information.

- Misinformation: Spread of false information through media channels undermines public trust and distorts perceptions.

6. Challenges and Ethical Considerations

Ethical Standards:

- Media Responsibility: Upholding journalistic ethics and standards in reporting promotes accurate and unbiased information.

- Sensationalism: Balancing between informative reporting and sensationalized content that distorts public perception.

The influence of media on public perception is profound and multifaceted, impacting political discourse, social attitudes, and public trust. Understanding the dynamics of media influence helps navigate its role in shaping societal narratives and fostering informed public engagement.

Engaging with the American Public

Effective communication is crucial for any successful political agenda, including Project 2025 of the Heritage Foundation and Donald Trump's Agenda 47. These strategies aim to ensure that policy initiatives are clearly articulated, understood, and supported by the public. This in-depth analysis covers various aspects of effective communication, including message development, audience engagement, media utilization, and feedback mechanisms.

1. Message Development

Clarity and Consistency:

- **Clear Objectives**: Clearly define the goals of Project 2025 and Agenda 47. This includes outlining specific policies, expected outcomes, and the steps required to achieve these goals.

- **Consistent Messaging**: Maintain consistency across all communication channels. This helps reinforce the message and avoids confusion among the audience.

Framing and Narrative:

- **Effective Framing**: Frame the message in a way that resonates with the audience's values and concerns. For instance, emphasize economic growth, job creation, and national security to appeal to a broad base.

- **Compelling Narratives**: Use storytelling to make complex policy issues relatable. Highlight personal stories and case studies that illustrate the impact of the proposed policies.

Simple and Direct Language:

- **Avoid Jargon**: Use language that is easily understood by the general public. Avoid technical jargon and bureaucratic terms.

- **Clear and Direct**: Communicate in a straightforward manner, making it easy for the audience to grasp the key points.

2. Audience Engagement

Understanding the Audience:

- **Demographic Analysis**: Identify key demographics and tailor messages to address their specific interests and concerns. This includes age, gender, geographic location, and political affiliation.

- **Psychographic Insights**: Understand the values, beliefs, and motivations of the target audience. This helps in crafting messages that resonate on a deeper level.

Personalized Communication:

- **Segmented Messaging**: Develop different messages for different segments of the audience. For example, emphasize economic policies for business owners and healthcare reforms for seniors.

- **Interactive Platforms**: Use social media and other digital platforms to engage with the audience directly. Encourage questions, comments, and feedback to foster a sense of involvement.

Two-Way Communication:

- **Engagement Mechanisms**: Create opportunities for dialogue and interaction. This can include town hall meetings, Q&A sessions, and online forums.

- **Listening to Feedback**: Actively listen to the audience's feedback and concerns. This helps in refining the message and addressing any misunderstandings.

3. Media Utilization

Traditional Media:

- **Press Releases**: Use press releases to disseminate important information to a wide audience. Ensure they are well-written and highlight key points.

- **Media Interviews**: Leverage media interviews to reach a broader audience. Prepare spokespersons with key talking points and anticipated questions.

Digital Media:

- **Social Media**: Utilize social media platforms such as Twitter, Facebook, and Instagram to share updates, engage with followers, and amplify the message. Use hashtags, multimedia content, and interactive features to increase engagement.

- **Email Campaigns**: Implement targeted email campaigns to keep supporters informed and mobilized. Personalize emails to increase relevance and open rates.

Owned Media:

- **Websites and Blogs**: Maintain an official website and blog to provide detailed information about Project 2025 and Agenda 47. Use these platforms to publish articles, policy papers, and updates.

- **Podcasts and Videos**: Create podcasts and videos to reach a wider audience. These formats are particularly effective for explaining complex issues in an engaging way.

---

4. Feedback Mechanisms

Surveys and Polls:

- **Regular Surveys**: Conduct regular surveys to gauge public opinion on various aspects of the policies. Use the data to adjust messaging and address any areas of concern.

- **Poll Analysis**: Analyze poll results to understand trends and shifts in public perception. This helps in identifying which messages are resonating and which need to be adjusted.

Focus Groups:

- **Targeted Focus Groups**: Organize focus groups with different segments of the audience to gain qualitative insights. This helps in understanding the nuances of public opinion.

- **Discussion Analysis**: Analyze discussions from focus groups to identify common themes, concerns, and suggestions. Use this information to refine communication strategies.

Open Forums:

- **Public Forums**: Host public forums to discuss key issues and gather feedback. These forums provide a platform for direct interaction with the audience.

- **Online Discussions**: Facilitate online discussions on social media platforms and dedicated forums. Encourage open dialogue and respond to comments and questions.

---

5. Overcoming Communication Barriers

Addressing Misinformation:

- **Fact-Checking**: Implement robust fact-checking mechanisms to counter misinformation. Provide clear and accurate information to dispel myths and falsehoods.

- **Proactive Communication**: Proactively address potential misunderstandings and clarify complex issues before they become sources of confusion.

Building Trust:

- **Transparency**: Be transparent about the goals, processes, and outcomes of the policies. This helps in building trust with the audience.

- **Credibility**: Use credible sources and authoritative voices to support the message. This enhances the legitimacy of the communication.

Adapting to Cultural Sensitivities:

- **Cultural Awareness**: Be aware of cultural differences and sensitivities when communicating with diverse audiences. Tailor messages to respect cultural norms and values.

- **Inclusive Language**: Use inclusive language that resonates with all segments of the population. Avoid language that could be perceived as exclusionary or discriminatory.

Effective communication is a cornerstone of successful policy implementation for both Project 2025 and Agenda 47. By developing clear and consistent messages, engaging with the audience, utilizing various media channels, and establishing robust feedback mechanisms, these initiatives can ensure their goals are understood and supported by the public. Overcoming communication barriers and building trust are essential for fostering a positive public perception and achieving the desired outcomes.

Chapter 12   Challenges and Criticisms
Political Opposition and Public Dissent

P olitical opposition and public dissent are vital components of democratic systems, playing a crucial role in shaping, challenging, and refining significant policy initiatives such as Project 2025 of the Heritage Foundation and Donald Trump's Agenda 47. These forms of resistance arise from various sectors of society, driven by ideological differences, interest group lobbying, and grassroots activism. This detailed exploration delves into the origins, methods, impacts, and strategies for managing political opposition and public dissent within the context of these two major policy frameworks.

1. Origins of Opposition

Ideological Divergence:

- **Political Ideologies:** Opposition often stems from fundamental ideological differences. Progressive and liberal factions may resist the conservative agendas of Project 2025 and Agenda 47, advocating for policies that emphasize social welfare, environmental protection, and economic equality.

- **Value Conflicts:** Core values such as civil liberties, social justice, and economic inclusivity can clash with the principles underpinning conservative policy proposals, leading to vocal and organized resistance.

Interest Groups and Advocacy Organizations:

- **Economic Stakeholders:** Businesses and industries potentially affected by regulatory changes, tax reforms, or healthcare policies can mobilize against these initiatives. For instance, environmental regulations proposed by Project 2025 might face opposition from energy and manufacturing sectors.

- **Social Advocacy Groups:** Organizations focused on civil rights, environmental protection, healthcare access, and other social issues often challenge policies that they perceive as detrimental to their causes.

Political Rivals:

- **Party Politics:** Democratic politicians and liberal factions typically oppose conservative policies to maintain their political base and challenge Republican dominance.

- **Electoral Strategies:** Political opponents use policy critiques to galvanize their supporters and influence electoral outcomes, often framing their resistance as part of broader campaign strategies.

2. Methods of Dissent

Public Demonstrations and Protests:

- **Grassroots Mobilization:** Grassroots movements leverage social media and community networks to organize large-scale protests, rallies, and demonstrations. These events draw public and media attention, amplifying dissent.

- **Symbolic Actions:** Sit-ins, marches, and other forms of peaceful protest serve as powerful symbols of resistance, rallying support and drawing attention to specific issues.

Media Campaigns:

- **Traditional Media:** Newspapers, television, and radio provide platforms for publicizing opposition viewpoints. Opinion pieces, investigative reports, and editorials critically analyze policy proposals and highlight potential negative impacts.

- **Digital Platforms:** Social media, blogs, and online news sites enable rapid dissemination of dissenting opinions. Hashtags, viral posts, and online petitions mobilize public support and create pressure on policymakers.

Legal Challenges:

- **Litigation:** Opponents may file lawsuits to contest the legality or constitutionality of specific policies. Legal battles can delay implementation and bring issues before the judiciary, where they receive further scrutiny.

- **Amicus Briefs:** Advocacy groups and organizations submit amicus briefs in court cases, providing expert opinions and arguments to support their positions.

Legislative Actions:

- **Opposition Bills and Amendments:** Politicians introduce counter-legislation, amendments, or resolutions to challenge or modify proposed policies. These actions can create legislative hurdles and slow down policy implementation.

- **Public Hearings:** Legislative committees hold public hearings to gather testimonies from experts, stakeholders, and citizens. These hearings provide a forum for airing dissenting views and discussing the implications of policy proposals.

3. Impacts of Opposition and Dissent

Policy Modifications and Compromises:

- **Revisions and Amendments:** Sustained opposition can lead to significant policy revisions or compromises. Policymakers may adjust proposals to address concerns and garner broader support.

- **Incremental Implementation:** Faced with strong resistance, policymakers might implement changes incrementally, allowing time to address issues and build consensus.

Public Perception and Awareness:

- **Increased Awareness:** Opposition movements raise public awareness about the details and potential consequences of policy proposals. This can lead to more informed public debate and citizen engagement.

- **Negative Perception:** Intense dissent can create negative perceptions of policies and their proponents, impacting public trust and support.

Political Consequences:

- **Electoral Impact:** Public dissent can influence electoral outcomes by shaping voter opinions and preferences. Candidates who align with opposition views may gain support, while those associated with contentious policies may face electoral challenges.

- **Policy Legitimacy:** Effective management of opposition can enhance the legitimacy and acceptance of policies. Conversely, poorly handled dissent can undermine policy credibility and implementation efforts.

4. Strategies for Managing and Addressing Dissent

Engagement and Dialogue:

- **Inclusive Dialogues:** Policymakers should engage with opponents through public consultations, town halls, and stakeholder meetings. Constructive dialogue fosters understanding and helps identify common ground.

- **Transparent Communication:** Clear and transparent communication about policy goals, processes, and expected outcomes builds trust and counters misinformation.

Compromise and Adaptation:

- **Policy Adjustments:** Being open to modifying policies in response to valid concerns demonstrates flexibility and a willingness to collaborate. This can reduce resistance and build broader support.

- **Phased Implementation:** Implementing policies in phases allows for adjustments based on feedback and minimizes disruption, making it easier to address concerns as they arise.

Public Education and Advocacy:

- **Information Campaigns:** Conducting information campaigns to explain the benefits and rationale behind policies helps build public support. Using data, case studies, and expert endorsements can strengthen these efforts.

- **Advocacy Networks:** Mobilizing support from advocacy networks and allies helps counter opposition narratives and reinforce the policy agenda.

Legal and Political Maneuvering:

- **Robust Legal Defense:** Preparing strong legal defenses to counter lawsuits and challenges is essential. Engaging expert legal counsel ensures effective navigation of judicial processes.

- **Political Alliances:** Building coalitions and alliances across party lines strengthens support and reduces the impact of opposition. Collaborative efforts enhance policy resilience and implementation.

Political opposition and public dissent are essential to the democratic process, influencing the development and refinement of significant policy initiatives like Project 2025 and Agenda 47. By understanding the origins, methods, and impacts of opposition, policymakers can develop strategies to manage dissent effectively, engage constructively with critics, and ensure successful policy implementation. Addressing concerns transparently, adapting policies as needed, and fostering inclusive dialogue are key to building broad-based support and achieving policy objectives.

Addressing Criticisms and Misconceptions

ddressing criticisms and misconceptions is crucial for the success and public acceptance of significant policy initiatives such as Project 2025 of the Heritage Foundation and Donald Trump's Agenda 47. This in-depth exploration covers the nature of these criticisms, common misconceptions, and strategies to effectively counter them. It also examines how addressing these issues can enhance the credibility and effectiveness of these initiatives.

1. Nature of Criticisms

Ideological Opposition:

- **Progressive Critiques:** Many criticisms stem from ideological differences, with progressives often opposing conservative policies for their perceived impact on social justice, environmental protection, and economic equality.

- **Libertarian Concerns:** Libertarians might criticize aspects of Project 2025 and Agenda 47 that they view as expanding government intervention or compromising individual freedoms.

Policy Specific Concerns:

- **Economic Impact:** Critics argue that certain economic policies, such as tax cuts for the wealthy or deregulation, could increase income inequality and harm the middle class.

- **Environmental Issues:** Environmental advocates may criticize policies that prioritize economic growth over environmental sustainability, arguing they could exacerbate climate change and harm natural ecosystems.

Social and Cultural Criticisms:

- **Healthcare and Social Services:** Policies perceived to undermine healthcare access, education funding, or social services for marginalized groups often face significant criticism.

- **Cultural Impact:** Critics may argue that certain policies could erode cultural diversity and inclusivity, potentially marginalizing minority communities.

2. Common Misconceptions

Misunderstanding of Objectives:

- **Economic Policies:** There is often a misconception that economic policies favor only the wealthy or large corporations. In reality, proponents argue these policies aim to stimulate overall economic growth, job creation, and innovation.

- **Regulatory Changes:** Deregulation is sometimes misunderstood as eliminating necessary protections. However, supporters contend it is about removing unnecessary burdens that stifle economic activity.

Impact on Social Services:

- **Healthcare Reforms:** Critics may mistakenly believe that healthcare reforms will reduce access to care. Proponents argue that reforms aim to increase efficiency, reduce costs, and improve quality of care.

- **Education Policies:** Misconceptions about education policies may include fears of reduced funding or support. In contrast, the goal is often to enhance educational outcomes through innovation and efficiency.

Environmental Misconceptions:

- **Sustainability Initiatives:** Critics may believe that policies ignore environmental sustainability. However, both Project 2025 and Agenda 47 include measures to promote energy independence and innovation, which can contribute to sustainable practices.

3. Strategies to Address Criticisms and Misconceptions

Transparent Communication:

- **Clear Messaging:** Clearly articulate the goals, benefits, and long-term vision of policies to the public. Use accessible language and concrete examples to explain complex policy issues.

- **Open Dialogue:** Engage in open and honest dialogue with critics, stakeholders, and the public. Address concerns directly and provide evidence-based responses to counter misconceptions.

Data-Driven Responses:

- **Evidence-Based Policies:** Use data and research to support policy proposals. Share studies, statistics, and real-world examples that demonstrate the effectiveness and benefits of the policies.

- **Case Studies:** Highlight successful case studies from other regions or countries where similar policies have led to positive outcomes.

Engagement with Stakeholders:

- **Inclusive Consultations:** Involve a broad range of stakeholders in the policy development process. This includes industry leaders, community organizations, and advocacy groups who can provide valuable insights and help build consensus.

- **Advisory Committees:** Establish advisory committees comprising experts from various fields to review and provide input on policy proposals. This helps ensure policies are well-rounded and address multiple perspectives.

Educational Campaigns:

- **Public Education:** Launch educational campaigns to inform the public about the specifics of policies and their intended benefits. Use multimedia platforms to reach diverse audiences.

- **Workshops and Seminars:** Organize workshops, seminars, and town hall meetings to engage with communities, answer questions, and clarify misunderstandings.

Policy Adaptation and Flexibility:

- **Responsive Adjustments:** Be willing to adapt and modify policies based on feedback and emerging evidence. This demonstrates responsiveness and a commitment to achieving the best outcomes.

- **Phased Implementation:** Implement policies in phases, allowing for assessment and adjustments as needed. This approach helps address concerns incrementally and build trust over time.

Building Alliances:

- **Coalition Building:** Form alliances with like-minded organizations, political allies, and thought leaders to support and advocate for the policies. A united front strengthens the credibility and reach of policy initiatives.

- **Grassroots Mobilization:** Mobilize grassroots supporters to advocate for the policies within their communities. Personal stories and local advocacy can effectively counter misconceptions and build public support.

Legal and Legislative Strategies:

- **Robust Legal Framework:** Ensure policies are backed by a strong legal framework to withstand challenges. Engage legal experts to review and defend policies against potential lawsuits.

- **Legislative Advocacy:** Work closely with legislators to secure support and passage of policy measures. Provide lawmakers with the information and resources they need to advocate effectively.

4. Enhancing Credibility and Effectiveness

Continuous Evaluation:

- **Performance Metrics:** Establish clear metrics for evaluating the success and impact of policies. Regularly review and report on these metrics to demonstrate accountability and progress.

- **Independent Reviews:** Commission independent reviews and audits of policy implementation. Transparency in evaluation enhances credibility and trust.

Public Feedback Mechanisms:

- **Feedback Channels:** Create channels for the public to provide feedback and suggestions. Actively seek out and incorporate this feedback into policy refinement.

- **Citizen Panels:** Form citizen panels to review policies and provide grassroots perspectives. This ensures policies are grounded in the realities and needs of the population.

Media Engagement:

- **Proactive Media Relations:** Engage proactively with the media to ensure accurate reporting on policy initiatives. Provide journalists with detailed information, press releases, and access to experts.

- **Countering Misinformation:** Actively counter misinformation and false narratives through fact-checking and timely responses. Use social media and other platforms to reach a wide audience.

Addressing criticisms and misconceptions is essential for the successful implementation of Project 2025 and Agenda 47. By understanding the origins of opposition, clarifying misconceptions, and employing strategic responses, policymakers can enhance the credibility, acceptance, and effectiveness of these initiatives. Transparent communication, stakeholder engagement, educational campaigns, and continuous evaluation are key to building broad-based support and ensuring the long-term success of these policy frameworks.

Overcoming Legislative and Bureaucratic Hurdles

Overcoming legislative and bureaucratic hurdles is a critical aspect of implementing ambitious policy initiatives such as Project 2025 of the Heritage Foundation and Donald Trump's Agenda 47. This detailed exploration delves into the challenges posed by legislative processes and bureaucratic inertia, strategies for navigating these obstacles, and the importance of effective governance in achieving policy goals.

1. Understanding Legislative and Bureaucratic Challenges

Legislative Hurdles:

- **Partisan Gridlock:** The highly polarized nature of contemporary politics can result in legislative gridlock, where significant policy proposals face stiff opposition and slow progress through Congress.

- **Committee Bottlenecks:** Key legislation often gets stalled in congressional committees, where it can be subjected to extensive scrutiny, amendments, or even indefinite delays.

- **Lobbying and Special Interests:** Powerful lobbying groups and special interest organizations can exert significant influence over legislators, potentially obstructing policies that do not align with their agendas.

Bureaucratic Inertia:

- **Complex Regulatory Environment:** Navigating the intricate web of federal regulations and procedures can be daunting, leading to delays and complications in policy implementation.

- **Institutional Resistance:** Government agencies may resist changes that disrupt established routines, threaten budgets, or require significant adjustments in operations.

- **Resource Constraints:** Limited financial, human, and technological resources can impede the effective execution of new policies, particularly those requiring extensive coordination and new infrastructure.

2. Strategies for Overcoming Legislative Hurdles

Building Bipartisan Support:

- **Coalition Building:** Forming coalitions with legislators across the political spectrum can help garner broader support for policy proposals. This involves finding common ground and crafting policies that address the concerns of both parties.

- **Targeted Advocacy:** Engaging in targeted advocacy efforts to educate and persuade key legislators about the benefits and necessity of the proposed policies. This includes providing them with data, case studies, and constituent testimonials.

Effective Legislative Tactics:

- **Strategic Timing:** Introducing legislation at opportune moments, such as during periods of high public support or following relevant events, can increase the likelihood of successful passage.

- **Incremental Approaches:** When comprehensive reforms face significant opposition, adopting incremental approaches can facilitate progress. This involves breaking down large initiatives into smaller, more manageable pieces of legislation.

Engaging Public Support:

- **Grassroots Mobilization:** Mobilizing grassroots support through public campaigns, town halls, and social media can put pressure on legislators to act in favor of the proposed policies.

- **Media Outreach:** Utilizing media platforms to highlight the benefits of the policies and address any misinformation or concerns. This helps shape public opinion and generate a favorable environment for legislative action.

3. Strategies for Navigating Bureaucratic Hurdles

Streamlining Processes:

- **Regulatory Reform:** Advocating for regulatory reforms that simplify and streamline processes, reduce red tape, and enhance efficiency. This may involve revising outdated regulations and adopting best practices from other jurisdictions.

- **Interagency Coordination:** Promoting better coordination among government agencies to ensure a unified and efficient approach to policy implementation. Establishing interagency task forces can facilitate collaboration and information sharing.

Enhancing Administrative Capacity:

- **Resource Allocation:** Securing adequate funding and resources to support the implementation of new policies. This includes investing in technology, training, and hiring additional personnel where necessary.

- **Capacity Building:** Providing training and capacity-building programs for government employees to equip them with the skills and knowledge needed to effectively implement and manage new policies.

Overcoming Institutional Resistance:

- **Change Management:** Implementing change management strategies to address resistance within government agencies. This includes engaging employees in the planning process, addressing their concerns, and demonstrating the benefits of the proposed changes.

- **Leadership and Vision:** Strong leadership is essential to overcome bureaucratic inertia. Appointing dynamic leaders who are committed to the policy goals and capable of driving change can significantly enhance the chances of successful implementation.

4. Importance of Effective Governance

Transparent Governance:

- **Accountability Mechanisms:** Establishing robust accountability mechanisms to ensure transparency and integrity in the implementation process. This includes regular audits, public reporting, and independent oversight.

- **Stakeholder Engagement:** Engaging stakeholders, including civil society organizations, industry representatives, and community leaders, in the governance process. Their input and feedback can enhance the effectiveness and legitimacy of the policies.

Adaptive Governance:

- **Flexibility and Responsiveness:** Adopting a flexible and responsive approach to governance that allows for adjustments based on feedback, emerging challenges, and changing circumstances. This ensures policies remain relevant and effective.

- **Continuous Improvement:** Implementing mechanisms for continuous monitoring and evaluation of policies to identify areas for improvement. This involves using data and evidence to inform decision-making and policy adjustments.

Collaborative Governance:

- **Public-Private Partnerships:** Leveraging public-private partnerships to enhance resource mobilization, innovation, and implementation capacity. Collaboration with the private sector can bring additional expertise, technology, and funding.

- **International Cooperation:** Engaging in international cooperation and learning from the experiences of other countries can provide valuable insights and best practices for overcoming legislative and bureaucratic hurdles.

Overcoming legislative and bureaucratic hurdles is essential for the successful implementation of Project 2025 and Agenda 47. By understanding the nature of these challenges and employing strategic approaches, policymakers can navigate the complexities of the legislative process and bureaucratic environment. Building bipartisan support, engaging public and stakeholder support, streamlining processes, and enhancing governance are key strategies for ensuring the effective execution of ambitious policy initiatives. Through transparent, adaptive, and collaborative governance, these initiatives can achieve their intended goals and contribute to the broader vision of economic growth, national security, and societal well-being.

Chapter 13   Future Outlook
Long-term Vision and Sustainability

Long-term vision and sustainability are foundational to the success of any extensive policy initiative. Project 2025, proposed by the Heritage Foundation, and Agenda 47, envisioned by Donald Trump, both emphasize the necessity for strategic foresight and sustainable practices to ensure a lasting impact on the United States. This detailed exploration delves into the principles, strategies, and key components of long-term vision and sustainability, highlighting their significance in shaping a prosperous and resilient future.

1. Understanding Long-term Vision and Sustainability

- **Strategic Planning:** A long-term vision requires comprehensive strategic planning that outlines clear goals, milestones, and actionable steps over an extended period. This involves anticipating future trends, challenges, and opportunities.

- **Intergenerational Equity:** Ensuring that the benefits of current policies and initiatives extend to future generations. This principle underscores the importance of creating lasting value and avoiding short-termism.

- **Holistic Approach:** A broad and inclusive perspective that considers economic, social, and environmental dimensions. This approach ensures that policies are balanced and address the multifaceted nature of sustainability.

Sustainability

- **Environmental Stewardship:** Implementing practices that protect and preserve natural resources, reduce environmental impact, and promote ecological balance.

- **Economic Viability:** Ensuring that economic growth and development are financially sustainable, providing stable and enduring benefits to society.

- **Social Responsibility:** Addressing social needs and promoting equity, inclusion, and community well-being as integral components of sustainable development.

2. Strategic Components of Long-term Vision and Sustainability

Economic Strategies

- **Innovation and Technology:** Investing in research and development to drive innovation and technological advancements. This includes fostering an environment that supports startups, encourages entrepreneurship, and promotes cutting-edge industries.

- **Diversified Economy:** Developing a diversified economic base that reduces dependence on any single sector. This enhances resilience against economic shocks and creates a stable economic environment.

- **Infrastructure Development:** Investing in robust and modern infrastructure to support economic activities and improve quality of life. This includes transportation, energy, telecommunications, and water management systems.

Environmental Strategies

- **Renewable Energy:** Transitioning to renewable energy sources to reduce carbon emissions and dependence on fossil fuels. This includes solar, wind, hydro, and geothermal energy.

- **Conservation Efforts:** Protecting natural habitats, biodiversity, and ecosystems through conservation programs and sustainable land use practices.

- **Pollution Control:** Implementing stringent regulations and technologies to minimize pollution and its impact on air, water, and soil quality.

Social Strategies

- **Education and Workforce Development:** Ensuring access to quality education and continuous learning opportunities to prepare a skilled and adaptable workforce.

- **Healthcare Access:** Providing affordable and comprehensive healthcare services to promote public health and well-being.

- **Community Development:** Investing in community infrastructure, affordable housing, and social services to enhance living standards and social cohesion.

3. Project 2025 and Agenda 47: Integrating Long-term Vision and Sustainability

- **Policy Framework:** Project 2025 outlines a comprehensive policy framework designed to achieve sustainable economic growth, environmental protection, and social well-being. It emphasizes conservative principles, such as limited government, free-market economy, and individual liberties.

- **Strategic Initiatives:** Key initiatives include tax reforms to stimulate economic activity, deregulation to reduce bureaucratic burdens, and investments in technology and innovation.

- **Environmental Policies:** Project 2025 promotes sustainable environmental practices, including support for renewable energy and conservation efforts.

Agenda 47

- **Economic Reforms:** Agenda 47 focuses on revitalizing the American economy through tax cuts, deregulation, and infrastructure investments. It aims to create jobs, boost economic growth, and enhance global competitiveness.

- **Energy Independence:** A significant aspect of Agenda 47 is achieving energy independence by promoting domestic energy production, including oil, natural gas, and renewables.

- **National Security:** Strengthening national security through military modernization, border security, and cybersecurity initiatives is a core component of Agenda 47.

4. Synergies Between Project 2025 and Agenda 47

Common Goals:

- Both initiatives aim to stimulate economic growth, create jobs, and enhance national security. They emphasize the importance of innovation, technology, and infrastructure development.

- Environmental sustainability is a shared priority, with a focus on renewable energy and conservation efforts.

Collaborative Strategies

- **Policy Integration:** Combining the policy frameworks of Project 2025 and Agenda 47 to create a cohesive and comprehensive approach to national development.

- **Public-Private Partnerships:** Leveraging public-private partnerships to fund and implement key projects in infrastructure, technology, and environmental conservation.

- **Bipartisan Support:** Building bipartisan support to ensure the successful implementation and longevity of policies.

5. Challenges and Considerations

Economic Challenges:

- Balancing short-term economic gains with long-term sustainability requires careful planning and execution. Policies must be designed to avoid creating economic disparities and social inequities.

Environmental Challenges:

- Achieving environmental sustainability involves addressing climate change, reducing carbon emissions, and protecting natural resources. This requires international cooperation and adherence to global environmental standards.

Social Challenges:

- Ensuring social inclusion and equity in the face of rapid economic and technological changes is crucial. Policies must address the needs of vulnerable populations and promote social justice.

Long-term vision and sustainability are essential for the success of Project 2025 and Agenda 47. By integrating comprehensive economic, environmental, and social strategies, these initiatives aim to create a prosperous, resilient, and sustainable future for the United States. Addressing the challenges and leveraging the synergies between Project 2025 and Agenda 47 can pave the way for a balanced and enduring development path that benefits current and future generations.

Projected Outcomes and Success Metrics

The success of comprehensive policy initiatives like Project 2025 by the Heritage Foundation and Agenda 47 envisioned by Donald Trump is determined by clearly defined projected outcomes and success metrics. This detailed exploration delves into the anticipated outcomes, the criteria for measuring success, and the significance of these metrics in evaluating the effectiveness of the proposed policies.

1. Understanding Projected Outcomes and Success Metrics

Projected Outcomes

- **Economic Growth:** Anticipated increases in GDP, employment rates, and productivity resulting from policy implementations.

- **Social Improvements:** Enhancements in quality of life, including better healthcare, education, and social services.

- **Environmental Benefits:** Positive impacts on environmental sustainability, including reductions in carbon emissions and improvements in air and water quality.

- **National Security:** Strengthening national defense, cybersecurity, and border security.

Success Metrics

- **Quantitative Metrics:** Measurable indicators such as economic data, environmental statistics, and social indices.

- **Qualitative Metrics:** Subjective evaluations including public opinion, expert assessments, and international rankings.

- **Benchmarking:** Comparing performance against predefined targets or historical data to assess progress.

2. Projected Outcomes and Success Metrics for Project 2025

Economic Outcomes

- **GDP Growth:** Projected annual GDP growth rates as a result of tax reforms, deregulation, and innovation incentives.

- **Job Creation:** Number of jobs created in key sectors such as technology, manufacturing, and services.

- **Investment Levels:** Increases in domestic and foreign investments driven by favorable economic policies.

Social Outcomes

- **Healthcare Access:** Improvements in healthcare coverage, affordability, and health outcomes.

- **Educational Attainment:** Increases in graduation rates, literacy levels, and vocational training enrollments.

- **Poverty Reduction:** Reductions in poverty rates and improvements in income distribution.

Environmental Outcomes:

- **Renewable Energy Adoption:** Percentage increase in the use of renewable energy sources.

- **Carbon Emission Reductions:** Measurable decreases in greenhouse gas emissions.

- **Conservation Success:** Area of land and water bodies protected and restored.

National Security Outcomes

- **Military Readiness:** Enhancements in military capabilities and readiness.

- **Cybersecurity Improvements:** Reductions in cyber threats and successful defense against cyber attacks.

- **Border Security:** Increases in border security measures and reductions in illegal crossings.

Success Metrics

- **Economic Indicators:** GDP growth rate, unemployment rate, and inflation rate.

- **Social Indicators:** Healthcare coverage rate, education attainment levels, and poverty rate.

- **Environmental Indicators:** Carbon footprint, air and water quality indices, and biodiversity metrics.

- **Security Indicators:** Defense readiness levels, cybersecurity incident rates, and border security effectiveness.

3. Projected Outcomes and Success Metrics for Agenda 47

Economic Outcomes

- **Tax Revenue Growth:** Increases in tax revenues from economic expansion and improved compliance.

- **Business Growth:** Number of new businesses established and expansion of existing enterprises.

- **Infrastructure Development:** Scale and impact of infrastructure projects on economic activities.

Social Outcomes

- **Healthcare Improvements:** Better health outcomes and patient satisfaction rates.

- **Educational Advancements:** Higher educational achievement and improved school facilities.

- **Social Stability:** Reductions in crime rates and increases in community engagement.

Environmental Outcomes

- **Energy Independence:** Levels of domestic energy production and reduction in energy imports.

- **Environmental Protection:** Implementation of sustainable practices and reductions in pollution levels.

- **Climate Resilience:** Enhancements in infrastructure and communities' ability to withstand climate impacts.

National Security Outcomes

- **Military Strength:** Increases in defense spending and modernization of military equipment.

- **Homeland Security:** Improvements in homeland security measures and emergency response capabilities.

- **Global Influence:** Strengthening of international alliances and influence in global affairs.

Success Metrics

- **Economic Indicators:** Business growth rate, infrastructure investment levels, and tax revenue growth.

- **Social Indicators:** Health outcome indices, educational performance metrics, and crime rates.

- **Environmental Indicators:** Energy production statistics, pollution levels, and climate resilience scores.

- **Security Indicators:** Defense expenditure, homeland security readiness, and international influence rankings.

4. Integrated Success Metrics for Project 2025 and Agenda 47

Common Goals

- **Economic Prosperity:** Achieving sustained economic growth, job creation, and investment attraction.

- **Social Well-being:** Enhancing healthcare, education, and social services for all citizens.

- **Environmental Sustainability:** Promoting renewable energy, conservation efforts, and pollution control.

- **National Security:** Ensuring robust defense capabilities, cybersecurity, and border security.

Collaborative Metrics

- **Comprehensive Indicators:** Combining economic, social, environmental, and security metrics to provide a holistic view of success.

- **Public Satisfaction:** Measuring public approval ratings and satisfaction with government policies and services.

- **International Recognition:** Achieving positive assessments from international organizations and rankings.

5. Challenges and Considerations in Measuring Success

Economic Challenges

- **Data Accuracy:** Ensuring accurate and timely data collection and analysis to provide reliable metrics.

- **Economic Volatility:** Accounting for economic fluctuations and external shocks that may impact projected outcomes.

Environmental Challenges

- **Long-term Monitoring:** Establishing mechanisms for long-term environmental monitoring and evaluation.

- **Global Cooperation:** Coordinating with international efforts to address global environmental issues.

Social Challenges

- **Inclusive Metrics:** Developing metrics that capture the experiences and needs of diverse populations.

- **Equity Considerations:** Ensuring that success metrics reflect equitable outcomes for all segments of society.

Security Challenges

- **Dynamic Threats:** Adapting metrics to address evolving security threats and challenges.

- **Confidentiality:** Balancing the need for transparency with the confidentiality of security-related information.

Projected outcomes and success metrics are crucial for evaluating the effectiveness of Project 2025 and Agenda 47. By establishing clear goals and measurable indicators, these initiatives can ensure that their policies lead to sustained economic growth, social improvements, environmental sustainability, and enhanced national security. Addressing the challenges in measuring success and leveraging collaborative strategies will be key to achieving the long-term vision and sustainability envisioned by these comprehensive policy initiatives.

Conclusion
Recap of Key Points and The Path Forward

Project 2025 by the Heritage Foundation and Agenda 47 of Trump: The Path Forward for America

In this comprehensive recap, we revisit the essential elements and future trajectory outlined by Project 2025 of the Heritage Foundation and Agenda 47 envisioned by Donald Trump. This dive into details highlights the transformative potential, challenges, and strategic pathways shaping the future of American policy.

1. Vision and Objectives

Project 2025

- **Economic Prosperity:** Aimed at fostering robust economic growth through tax reforms, deregulation, and incentivizing innovation and entrepreneurship.

- **Social Advancement:** Focuses on enhancing healthcare access, improving educational outcomes, and addressing societal challenges through comprehensive reforms.

- **Environmental Sustainability:** Committed to promoting energy independence, sustainable practices, and environmental stewardship.

- **National Security:** Strengthening defense capabilities, cybersecurity measures, and border security to safeguard national interests.

Agenda 47

- **Economic Policies:** Emphasizes revitalizing industries, boosting job creation, and enhancing infrastructure to stimulate economic vitality.

- **Social Initiatives:** Prioritizes improving healthcare services, advancing educational opportunities, and fostering community resilience.

- **Environmental Commitment:** Aims for energy independence, promoting clean energy technologies, and preserving natural resources.

- **National Defense:** Focuses on bolstering military readiness, enhancing cybersecurity defenses, and reinforcing homeland security.

2. Strategic Implementation

Project 2025

- **Policy Framework:** Detailed policy initiatives crafted to address specific economic, social, environmental, and security challenges.

- **Legislative Support:** Collaborative efforts with lawmakers to enact supportive legislation and regulatory reforms.

- **Public Engagement:** Community outreach programs and public forums to garner support and address concerns.

Agenda 47

- **Executive Actions:** Utilization of executive orders and administrative directives to expedite policy implementation.

- **Congressional Alignment:** Working closely with Congress to pass legislative measures crucial for policy realization.

- **Stakeholder Collaboration:** Engaging stakeholders, including business leaders, advocacy groups, and local communities, to ensure inclusive policy outcomes.

3. Challenges and Considerations

Common Challenges

- **Political Opposition:** Navigating partisan divides and ideological differences to garner bipartisan support.

- **Economic Realities:** Addressing economic fluctuations and global market dynamics impacting policy outcomes.

- **Environmental Concerns:** Balancing economic growth with environmental sustainability and conservation efforts.

- **Security Imperatives:** Adapting to evolving security threats and safeguarding national interests effectively.

4. Roadmap for Success

Integrated Approach

- **Measurable Goals:** Defining clear success metrics across economic, social, environmental, and security domains.

- **Monitoring and Evaluation:** Establishing robust monitoring mechanisms to track progress and adjust strategies as needed.

- **Public Accountability:** Committing to transparency and accountability in policy implementation and outcomes.

Collaborative Strategies:

- **Public-Private Partnerships:** Leveraging private sector investments and expertise to amplify policy impact.

- **International Engagement:** Strengthening diplomatic ties and international cooperation on shared challenges.

- **Long-term Vision:** Sustaining momentum through long-term planning and strategic foresight to achieve enduring national benefits.

5. The Path Forward for America

Conclusion

- **Shared Vision:** Aligning national priorities with the aspirations and needs of the American people.

- **Resilient Strategies:** Building resilience against emerging challenges and global uncertainties.

- **Inclusive Growth:** Promoting equitable opportunities and inclusive growth across all sectors of society.

- **Legacy of Leadership:** Upholding America's leadership role in global affairs and advancing principles of freedom, democracy, and prosperity.

In conclusion, the path forward for America under Project 2025 and Agenda 47 hinges on concerted efforts to realize transformative policies that ensure economic vitality, social progress, environmental sustainability, and national security. By navigating challenges with strategic foresight and collaborative spirit, these initiatives aim to shape a future where America continues to thrive and lead on the global stage.

Made in the USA
Columbia, SC
25 September 2024

43047890R00098